Take Care
Tips

How to Care for Yourself
While You're Taking Care of Others

Jennifer Antkowiak

PITTSBURGH

Take Care Tips

How to Care for Yourself While You're Taking Care of Others

ISBN-13: 978-0-9800288-5-0

Library of Congress Control Number: 2008933292
CIP information available upon request

First Edition, 2009

St. Lynn's Press • POB 18680 • Pittsburgh, PA 15236
412.466.0790 • www.stlynnspress.com

Typesetting – Holly Wensel, Network Printing Services
Cover design – Jeff Nicoll
Editors – Abby Dees, Catherine Dees

Printed in the United States of America
on recycled paper

This title and all of St. Lynn's Press books may be purchased for educational, business, or sales promotional use. For information please write:

Special Markets Department • St. Lynn's Press • POB 18680 • Pittsburgh, PA 15236

10 9 8 7 6 5 4 3 2 1

To those I am blessed to care for,
and for all of you who make
the time to care for those you love.

Table of Contents

Introduction

❦

HOW LONG HAS IT BEEN since you've done anything for yourself? I'm willing to bet it's been way too long. I want to help you. I know that you may not feel you have time to spend on yourself because you have other people and things that you want to take care of. I know that you even feel a little bit (or a lot) of guilt about devoting any time to yourself. I have been where you are. I didn't take care of myself, and I ended up with a kidney stone, chest pains, headaches and extra weight to prove it. And that was just the *physical* fallout.

What have I learned from this? I have learned that we all have the power within ourselves to stop the destructive cycles and re-start our lives in a healthy, positive way. I have learned that when you devote even just a few minutes of time to making these changes, everyone around you benefits, too.

As of right this minute, you have permission to take care of yourself. Tell anyone who gives you a hard time that your new friend Jen said that you must spend at least ten guilt-free minutes on yourself, every day.

If you're going to be throwing my name around like that, I guess I should tell you a little bit about myself (it might be embarrassing if someone asks for details about your new buddy and you have nothing to say). I am Jennifer Antkowiak. I care for my husband, five young children and an older step-daughter. I also care for my father-in-law, and I took care of my mother-in-law while she was dying of cancer.

Because I wanted and needed to spend more time taking care of my family, I made the decision to leave the security and regular paycheck of my 17-year career as a TV news anchor and reporter. In the process, I gave myself a few new "babies" to take care of: *jennifer Productions* is a company I founded, with a passionate mission of gathering and presenting information that can help to make life easier for busy women and families. It started with writing some articles, then came a magazine, then I jumped back into what I knew best – television, but this time with a much easier-to-manage schedule. I am executive producer and host of a weekly talk show. And then I realized that I could reach and hopefully help even more people with a web site, so at 2 o'clock one morning, with $147 and limited web site knowledge, I started *www.jenniferTVshow.com.* It has quickly grown, and now we share make-life-easier information with people around the world. With TV and web and print, we have a nice platform of accessibility, so that people can easily find us when they need us.

Although it sounds like a lot, the beauty and the blessing of it is that I am able to do most of my work from home. I feel more in control of my schedule now, and I try very hard to consistently carve out some time for myself. I can tell you from hard-won experience that devoting time to focus on just you is *not* a luxury, it's a *necessity*. If you don't take the time you need to keep yourself strong, there's really no way you will ever possibly be strong enough to take care of anyone else. It's really just that simple, but it's tough to stay focused on that while you are taking care of life's other responsibilities.

I've learned to think about caring for myself as a *process*. I don't get it right all the time. I still have nights when I don't get enough sleep, and I still have days when I don't stand firm on giving myself ten minutes to recharge.

Now, I know your story isn't exactly like mine, but I'll bet we've got a few things in common. I'll bet you're a juggler, too. You have seen how one thing can lead to another, and another. You are different things to different people, and you have probably seen that it's easy for who you are and what you need to get lost. Family first, job second, and you end up somewhere at the end of the line. I want to help move you up to the front again, because if you put yourself first, you will see that it's easier to manage the rest. With Take Care Tips you will see that you don't have to block out a lot of time to make that happen. Ten minutes, max, and in some cases no time at all.

Response from people like you fuels me. Sometimes, after my presentations on How to Care for Yourself While You're Taking Care of Others, I have been overwhelmed by people who come up to me to share their stories and ask for help:

The woman who pushed her mother in a wheelchair up to me – both of them in tears: "Look at her," the mother said to me. "She's young, she's beautiful. All she does is take care of me. She doesn't spend any time on herself. She needs to go out with friends and do things for herself. I feel so guilty that she has to take care of me like this." "Mom, I told you," the daughter said, giving me a teary glance, "I wouldn't want to be anywhere else. I want to take care of you. This is what I want to be doing." Then, to me, "Please help me to make her understand."

The out-of-breath, pink-cheeked man in a rumpled shirt who came running in, asking if he had missed my talk. When I told him he had, he asked if I had the information in a book, or on a DVD. "I need help," he told me – and again, some tears. "I live out of town, but I travel back here to take care of my mother. No one else in the family can do it, and to be honest, I don't know if I can do it either."

A woman who nervously and quietly told me, after I gave the presentation in a corporate setting, that she was taking care of a father with Alzheimer's. "I feel so guilty complaining about this," she whispered, "but it is really hard. I'm struggling to stay focused and keep up with everything here at work. I'm not sleeping. I'm gaining weight. I'm a mess. I need help."

How incredible that these people were willing to share this intensely emotional and personal information, just like that. I think it speaks to the desperate nature of caregivers – the very real, very urgent need for help.

Obviously, for each of these people, taking care of a loved one is the most important thing in their lives. However, as they were talking to me, I was worrying about who was taking care of *them*. In my own little world I have seen so many people walking around with those kinds of strong feelings right beneath the surface, unspoken and unattended-to. All it takes is for someone to open a door, or even just push it a little ajar, and they let everything go and cry for help. Others are walking around in a state of denial, adapting to the new stress levels as their new normal. This is not healthy. It will catch up with you. Caregivers need care too.

Sorry to break it to you, but it's not likely that a fairy is going to fly in with a magic wand and make everything better (I won't rule it out completely, I'm just saying it's not likely). So in the meantime, you're going to have to add taking care of yourself to your list of things to do. I don't have a magic wand, but I do have tools that will help.

Make no mistake, we are talking about serious subjects, personal crisis situations, actually (and we need to address them as such); but my way of thinking is you don't need one more heavy thing around you. I'm not going to scare you with tons of research and statistics (OK, well actually I am a little bit here and there, but it's all for the greater good!). Mostly, I'm going to give you practical information that you can use to re-energize your body and your brain, and get back to a feeling of happiness and wellbeing. Remember what that felt like?

Take Care Tips is organized into chapters that represent key areas of your life that you need to focus on to help you to reduce your risks of health problems specific to caregivers. You don't have to read this book cover to cover. I've set it up so that if you're having trouble sleeping, for example, you can flip to Chapter 5 and quickly get information that can help. Each chapter will also give you many ten-minute tips that you can start to use immediately. In a perfect world, we'd all have unlimited time, but I know first hand that here in Realityville time is a scarce, valuable commodity, especially when you're a caregiver. So...if you can commit to blocking out just ten little minutes (or even fewer), I'm going to teach you how you can make big, positive changes in your life. Along the way, you'll notice too that the areas of your life that you're going to need to focus on are related to things that your mother probably tried to get into your head all along. Let's look at them again, now that you're an adult. You'll see that some tips work best if you do them everyday, some are an every-once-in-a-while thing. You can decide what works best for you. That's the goal – no grading or stern looks from me. This book is like a big box of tools and I invite you to pick up and try out every single one.

You can do this. I am excited to be here with you. Time for you starts right now. Let's go.

one

Do Your Homework

I ***KNOW YOU DON'T HAVE THE TIME*** to read this book. I know you're busy. Stay with me though. I am so happy that you are doing this for yourself. Reading this shows that you have an awareness that things aren't right with the way that you're going through life right now. This is a big step towards regaining control over a routine that probably seems out of control much of the time.

Stop reading for just a minute. Close your eyes and take a deep breath in through your nose and let it out through your mouth. Let go of the stress of your day. Try to block out any other thing you think you should be doing right now.

I want you to think of your time with me as special time where you can focus on yourself. I want you to know that I am here to help you. I want you to relax, and to be comforted with the knowledge that you have everything you need inside yourself to take charge and manage any situation. Because you are immersed in so many other things, it might be hard for you to recognize that – and to see the power in that – right now. I will help you to understand that you must take care of yourself. I will help you to believe in your own strength.

I am extremely passionate about the messages in this book. Although honestly, it was difficult for me to find the time to focus on the work of writing it; the ideas and concepts were keeping me up at night. My own life-changing caregiving experiences have brought me to this path. It is my sincere hope and prayer that something that I have learned will help to make your life easier.

My Caregiving Story

I learned what it was like to be a caregiver at a young age. My mother lived with post-partum depression while I was growing up. Unfortunately, hers didn't get better with time. The disease was difficult for all of us to understand – my mom, my dad, and my three younger sisters and me. There were good days and bad days. It hurt me horribly to see the bad days. I know in my heart that my mom wanted to be happy and healthy for us and with us, and I'm afraid that she struggled and suffered even more than I know. It went on for years, with my mom seeing different doctors and staying in different facilities; and with all of us trying to hold down the fort in our own ways.

It was not the life either of my parents had envisioned, and when I was almost done with high school, my parents divorced. Because of my mother's illness, my sisters and I stayed in our house with my dad. My mom had moved in with her mom, about two hours away. She lived there for a couple of years before settling into an apartment back closer to my sisters.

By then, I had moved away to college, and throughout those years, besides being a student, I was a long-distance caregiver for my family – helping to relieve some of the pressure from my father, who was working and trying to raise us, and helping my mother and grandmother to manage my mom's care.

Not long after graduating from college, when I was working at a television station in Erie, Pennsylvania, I received a phone call from a police officer in my small home town, telling me that there had been an emergency – something with my mother – and that I needed to call the hospital. I called to check on what happened and after a long wait, an emergency room nurse came on the phone and told me, "Your mother is no longer with us." "You moved her to a different hospital?" I asked. "No, I'm sorry, she has passed," the nurse said.

Just like that. No more mother. I found out later that my mom had a heart attack. She was only 50 years old. It was sudden, and shocking, and final. I missed her immediately and deeply; but at the same time, I hoped that after living with a troubled mind for all of those years, my beautiful mother would find peace.

When my mom died I was three months away from getting married. We had been looking forward to going out together to shop for the dress she would wear to my wedding. Instead, here I was, in a daze, going though the motions of picking out clothes, flowers, prayers and songs for her funeral.

My mother-in-law-to-be offered me great support during that time. She scooped me up and took me under her wing. She had been orphaned as a child and she knew what it was like to move through life without a mother. She opened her heart to me and surrounded me with her love.

While I know my own mother watches and protects me from above, it was my mother-in-law who was physically here with me to celebrate my early career advancements, and later, for the births of four of our five children. She didn't live to see our last child come into this world.

Like my mother, my mother-in law (Me-ma, as I called her) was the ultimate caregiver, and never liked to admit if she was having any problems. Not long after my third son was born I noticed that she was short of breath at times, and seemed to be moving at a slower pace. She tried to dismiss it, but one afternoon she called me to say that she hated to bother me (of course) but she was having trouble catching her breath after doing some housework.

"What were you doing?" I asked. "Running up and down the stairs with laundry?"

"Making the bed," she answered.

She was out of breath after only making the bed. I asked her some questions and her responses sounded to me like they were coming from someone who was close to having a heart attack. I had to convince her to go to the emergency room. Doctors found several blockages. Me-ma went through quintuple bypass surgery and the long recovery period that followed.

Less than two years later, shortly after my daughter was born, I noticed that my mother-in-law wasn't eating much, and again seemed out of breath and slow at times. She confided in me that she had been having stomach pains and that she felt very tired. This time, doctors found cancer, a fast-growing kind. No surgery or therapy was recommended. We were told we should get in touch with Hospice.

When we went back to her house that sunny afternoon, Me-ma and I sat out on her screened porch (her favorite place) and we talked. "This is pretty bad, isn't it?" she asked. "Let's look at this as an adventure," I said hopefully. "Nobody knows how much time they have left, but let's make the most of it."

Through the years, Me-ma had seen how I kept my mother's memory close and her spirit alive, how I shared stories about her with my young children, how I asked her for help when I needed it, and how I felt her with me always. "Do you think it will be like that for you with me?" she asked. "I absolutely do," I said, and she smiled. "Please take care of Pap," she said.

Pap is my dear father-in-law, who lives with us now. "Of course I will," I told her. "I hate that all of this is on you," she said. "How am I going to repay you for all of this?" I held her hand and told her that my "payment" was the blessing of being with her – and her allowing me into this private time in her life.

"You know how they say that when you get up there, you can pull some strings, and help people?" she continued. "Well, if that's true, I want you to know that I will get with your mother and we will do whatever we can to help you...to make your life easier."

Six weeks from the cancer diagnosis, I gave the eulogy at my mother-in-law's funeral mass.

It was my honor and blessing to work with Hospice to take care of her during those six weeks. At the time it was happening, I was just back to work from my maternity leave – back to a full-time, extremely public job as a TV news anchor and reporter. I had three toddlers, an infant and a husband at home. In those last weeks I would stop at my in-laws' house on the way to work, on the way home, and then again after the kids were tucked into bed. I talked to doctors and looked online to find out everything I could about cancer and how it progresses. I researched medicines. I found myself administering medicines to my mother-in-law, keeping pain charts and lists of reactions to medications and dosages. I helped to organize counseling for family members. I kept a journal with my mother-in-law. I made sure my father-in-law was eating and sleeping. I tried to keep my house, and my in-laws' house, straightened up. I took care of my own family, and continued to breastfeed the baby. I tried to stay connected to what was going on in the world so that I could continue to do what I needed to do at work.

I had a strong sense that I was the one who needed to take care of all of these people and things, and I happily did them. I wouldn't have wanted it any other way. Looking back on it now though, I realize that I wasn't sleeping. I wasn't eating well. I wasn't getting any exercise. I gained weight. My skin was dry (I was probably dehydrated). I had aches and pains I never had before. I had headaches. But I kept moving.

Maybe because of my news background, researching what was happening consumed me. I know that knowledge is power, and I wanted to arm myself with as much knowledge as possible so that I could try to keep a step ahead of the situation. I didn't want to be caught off guard. I wanted to be able to remain a source of calm and strength to Me-ma and the family.

It wasn't until after my mother-in-law's funeral that I thought about myself. I was forced to. Not taking care of myself had caught up with me. I had to go to the hospital with chest pains – scared because of my family history of heart disease, including my mother dying of a heart attack at a young age. I had to stay overnight, hooked up to a heart monitor.

Thankfully, I checked out OK, but before the doctor released me, he asked me about my lifestyle. He told me to consider my chest pains as a big red flag to hit the brakes, and spend some time taking care of myself.

Looking at my little children's eyes when I got home fueled the power of the doctor's talk. My children were going to have to grow up without grandmothers, but I would do everything I could to make sure they did not have to grow up without me.

Early on, Hospice workers pointed out to me that by agreeing to be a caregiver, I was stepping into a role full of new challenges, and that these new challenges could cause a lot of mental and physical strain. "Don't worry about me, I'll be fine," I said.

How many times have you said, "Don't worry about me, I'll be fine"? As caregivers, we don't want to put a spotlight on ourselves. We don't want to think about our own health. We just don't have time. A Hospice doctor I interviewed for this book, Dr. Randy Hebert, who has done quite a bit of research on caregivers, brought out an interesting concept regarding the way we can think in this situation. When you are taking care of someone because they're sick – perhaps terminally ill – you feel sad. And you feel their sadness as well as your own, *because* you care so much. You feel depressed. Those are exactly the normal feelings you should be feeling. A loved one is sick or dying; how else would you feel? Asking you to feel positive, and to be motivated to be healthy is absolutely abnormal in that situation.

So, our challenge now is for you to find the strength to be abnormal (and even feel positive – but in an honest, realistic way). That "don't worry about me, I'll be fine" attitude isn't gonna cut it anymore. You have a lot of living to do. Don't allow caring for others to rob you of your health. Those you are caring for wouldn't want that, and I don't either.

From my own experience I know that it would have been tough if not impossible for someone to say something – anything – that could pull me away from my perceived responsibilities and "force" me to spend some time on myself.

Fact of life: When one caregiving situation is over, there are other people standing there who need your attention. If you wait for "leftover" time to begin taking care of yourself, it will never happen. You need to make time to take care of yourself now. You have me (and you know I'm fueled by the power of two strong, wonderful women) to help you.

Let me start by sharing some information about this already very personal, but also growing, public health issue.

Who is doing all of this caregiving?

Well, the short answer is, women who are not trained to be doing it. Stories like mine are being played out right now by at least 50 million people in America. Most of them are women. Most are older than me, in their mid to late 40s. Most have families and jobs. The majority of caregivers have a high school degree, and no formal health care training. Most have health problems of their own. Many have either lost or run the risk of losing their health insurance because their caregiving schedule forces them to either quit or reduce their hours of work outside the home. Most caregivers aren't getting the support they would like to be confident in caring for their loved ones. As the health care system becomes more and more strained, daily care is falling more and more on the shoulders of family caregivers. It's estimated that family caregivers are providing ongoing care to nearly 80% of the chronically ill in America.

There's huge economic impact to this situation as well.

Most family caregivers provide their services free of charge, but studies show that if all those caregivers were paid for their services – cooking, cleaning, administering medications, helping with basic hygiene, working out financial difficulties, managing health insurance, providing transportation, offering mental and physical help, etc. – they'd be earning nearly 300 billion dollars a year! These numbers are growing by the minute; they will continue to go up as our population continues to age (the numbers go up immediately if you agree with me that taking care of healthy people makes you a caregiver too).

Now, I'd guess that you're not that interested in putting a monetary value on your service, but still, it's nice to know. Those statistics speak loud and clear about the volume of volunteer caregiving. You are not alone. What you do is a big deal, remember that. Just be aware that while you're putting out all that time and energy looking after others, you could be taking a chance with your own health and wellbeing.

"I'll be fine." (Oh, really?)

When you're not taking care of your own health needs, you're putting yourself at higher risk – in some cases more than double the risk – for a variety of serious mental and physical diseases, as well as for dying younger. Many times the early signs and symptoms are there but the caregiver ignores them, making the problem more difficult to treat later on.

Medical research shows that those of us who are caregivers are almost twice as likely to develop heart disease and/or have a heart attack. We are almost twice as likely to develop diabetes, depression, and even cancer. We are more likely to be overweight or obese. We are also at risk for less serious diseases including chronic headaches, muscular pain, arthritis, colds and flu, and acid reflux.

These increased risks come directly as a result of the caregiving lifestyle. We aren't sleeping or eating well. Our stress levels are through the roof. Getting out to exercise just doesn't happen. Those negative patterns lead to problems with the immune system, and an increase in amount and severity of infections.

The stress alone involved with caregiving can take ten years off your life. Prolonged stress causes a variety of other problems in the body as well. Stress makes the heart and all the organs work harder. Caregivers are at a greater risk for developing high blood pressure.

This is scary stuff. I'm not telling you this to create more stress in your life. I'm telling you this because I want you to be aware of the facts regarding what you face if you continue with the routine you've created for yourself. The good news is, you absolutely have the power to turn things around and reduce your health risks. I am committed to helping you to do that.

Basic Medical Care for Caregivers

As we start, I want to go over some healthcare housekeeping tips with you. These are all things to check off or see to right away so that you will have a strong foundation for your new healthy lifestyle.

- Make sure your immunizations are up to date.
- Get your flu shot once a year (if you have questions or concerns ask your doctor).

- Take a daily multi-vitamin (ask your doctor or pharmacist if you have any questions about which formula would be best for you).
- Get a pneumonia vaccine.
- Get a tetanus booster every ten years.
- Get a yearly physical.
- Get the recommended cancer screenings based on your age and family history.
- Tell your doctor that you are a caregiver – this is so important. Saying this buzzword at the outset should send a strong message to your doctor, telling him or her to look at you in a different way. Saying that you're a caregiver will alert your doctor that you are dealing with higher than normal levels of stress, and that you need some extra care and attention. If you don't sense that is happening...get a new doctor!
- Tell your doctor if you're feeling depressed or nervous. Even if you wouldn't label yourself clinically depressed (a lot of us are and don't even know it), mention any sleeping or eating problems, or feelings of sadness, helplessness or hopelessness that don't go away. New therapies and medicines have made depression easier to treat. Don't be afraid of a diagnosis. Get help.

In the coming chapters, you will get information you need to be able to improve areas of your life that are important for total health and reduce your risks for problems down the road. Everything here is easy, practical, and achievable. The information comes from my own research and experience, as well as from the many experts I've had the pleasure of interviewing during my years in TV news and beyond.

In the Introduction I promised you my very best guilt-free ten minute tips to inspire you and to allow you to start feeling results right away – no matter what's going on in your caregiving life.

Let's start with some tips for setting and holding on to your personal goals. Even if you already know about these things, chances are good you're not living them. That's the case for most of us. After this, we'll talk about putting yourself in a new, energized state of mind.

Take Care Tip #1

Set Realistic Goals

CHANGING HABITS IS TRICKY STUFF. That's what we're working to do here. Change can seem intimidating, even when you are aware that you are trying to make a positive change. You're going to have to be willing to do it in baby steps. You're going to have to stick with it, even if today didn't go as well as you hoped. Don't think about trying to "snap out" of your present situation; instead, think about chipping away at feeling better one day – maybe even one minute – at a time. You will see and feel results and others will too, and that will help to keep you on track.

Our bodies and brains are amazing machines. When you start feeding them in a positive way, they will respond. Take ten minutes to think about just one goal that you'd like to achieve to take care of yourself. It could be about health and fitness, a creative project, relationships, spiritual development, time for reading, travel...anything. Set that thought and don't let it slip away.

Now... Take Yourself Off Hold

WHEN YOU FEEL LIKE YOUR LIFE GOALS are on hold it can be extremely frustrating. Get a grip on your priorities. Don't overwhelm yourself with too many things that you "absolutely have to get done" first. It's fine to focus on daily must-do items, but plan to do something that will move you even a little bit toward your long range goals. Holding on to your dreams and taking an active approach to achieving them will give you a fantastic feeling of control. That's the thought behind Tip #2.

Take ten minutes on a regular basis to keep a record of how you're doing as you progress toward your long term goal(s). Ideally, see if you can do this every day. Otherwise, just try to do it regularly. The more the better, of course, but anything that you can stick to is good. You can set up a Daily Priorities journal or notebook to help you stay on course.

Page 1 will be your reminder to yourself to keep an eye on the big picture, your life goals, as you move through each day. The daily pages will let you see how that's working for you.

Your page 1 could look like this:

MY TOP THREE LIFE GOALS ARE:

1. ______________________________
2. ______________________________
3. ______________________________

Your next pages could look like this:

TOP THREE THINGS I MUST ACCOMPLISH TODAY

Related to Work/Home:

1. ______________________________
2. ______________________________

Related to a Life Goal:

3. ______________________________

And then...

- Celebrate your accomplishments!
- Be grateful for the things that are going right today.
- Have confidence that you are exactly as strong as you need to be to handle whatever the day brings.

(You can celebrate these things even if you didn't find the time to write in your journal.)

Take Care Tip #3

Better Breathing

IT'S EASY TO GET INTO THE HABIT of shallow breathing, especially when we're concentrating on a task or just feeling overwhelmed. Better breathing is something I keep coming back to in my talks and in my own life, because simply taking the time to focus on getting a few good, deep breaths can change your body and your brain. The increased oxygen will give your brain a boost; it also helps to relax your muscles and your mind.

This is a great way to start your day, but any time is good. Find a few minutes to sit quietly. Place your feet flat on the floor. Rest your hands comfortably in your lap. Relax your shoulders. Close your eyes. Let everything else go and think only about your breathing. Breathe in slowly and deeply through your nose, counting while you do so. My friend, Health Psychologist Nancy Mramor, suggests making a mental note of the number of seconds you normally take for a breath. Hold that air in for a little bit, and then blow all of it out through your mouth. Observe how long that takes. Allow yourself to increase those numbers even by a second or two. Over time, you will increase your lung capacity. Taking a few minutes for deep breathing exercises like this will help you to relieve stress and re-energize for the rest of the day.

☛ *And When You're Done With That...*

Allow yourself to practice this kind of breathing as much as possible. At least once a day would be wonderful, and especially when you feel a lot of anxiety.

Take Care Tip #4

Accentuate the Positive

SOMETIMES WE CAN GET STUCK in our troubles, wallowing around in them with other people who are happy to wallow around with us. How helpful is that?

Clear the air of the negative energies. Take ten minutes right now to go through your address book and seek out positive people. Try to surround yourself with only happy, supportive friends and family members. Call one of these people and be so bold as to announce to them that you have realized that you haven't been doing enough to take care of yourself and you are working to change that. Ask them about their hobbies, and what they do to relieve stress. Chances are good that you will be surprised by the reaction. Maybe people have been wanting to reach out to you but didn't know how to start. Show them an open door.

Take Care Tip #5

Do Something You Used To Love To Do (Simple Pleasures)

INSTEAD OF COLLAPSING ON THE COUCH in front of the TV for a work break, take ten minutes to do something that feeds your inner child or your romantic self: Hold hands with someone you care about and go for a walk – or go play in the back yard with the kids. It doesn't have to be a whole afternoon; even a few minutes of doing something that brought you happiness in the past has a good chance of putting you back in touch with that sense of happiness again. And it can help create a positive frame of mind, making it easier for you to do things for yourself more often.

☛ *And When You're Done With That...*

Please do make it an afternoon. Allow yourself even more guilt-free time to go to a movie, a ballgame, or take a craft class. That may take some planning ahead, but do it for yourself. It can work wonders.

Take Care Tip #6

Keep Your Eye On The Prize

TAKE A FEW MINUTES to understand that when you're working to achieve an important goal (and yours is very important), you need to do everything in your power to stay focused on that goal. Realize that there will be bumps along the way to achieving your success. Accept the fact that those bumps are a normal part of the journey. Start to create an attitude that getting through those little challenges will only make you stronger and make your success even more rewarding.

two

Settle Yourself Down

❦

CAREGIVING AND STRESS go hand in hand. Stress can have so much negative impact in the body and the brain, it's important for us to figure out how to manage our stress so that we can relax.

Hang on to that idea for a minute. We're going to focus on managing – not eliminating – our stress. That's an important concept to get. Throughout our lives, bad things will happen. Throughout our lives, things we don't agree with will happen. That's a given. Many of those things will be out of our control. However, we do have the power to control our reactions to those things.

I try to teach my kids about this way of thinking, and sports seems to give me the opportunity to do it. You're playing basketball and the referee makes a bad call. What are you gonna do about it? Are you going to stomp and pout, and waste valuable game time with that behavior? Or, are you going to quickly accept (agree with it or not) that that's the call that was made, and now you have to use the time you have left to turn it to something positive?

How can you begin to manage stress in that powerful way? You have everything you need built right into you.

It's pretty much impossible to live a completely stress-free life, and even if it were possible, you probably wouldn't want to. Stress can be a positive influence in our lives by adding some urgency, energy, and excitement. But when we let that get out of control, the problems start.

What is stress, exactly?

The word stress represents the emotional and physical strain that happens in our bodies and our brains when we respond to pressure we feel around us.

Emotionally, we can respond to pressure by feeling tense, irritable, fatigued, or unfocused. Or sleepless. (We'll talk about insomnia in Chapter 5.)

Physically, stress can cause you to have a dry mouth, a fast, hard heartbeat, breathing problems, a sick stomach, sweaty palms, and tight, painful, sometimes jittery, muscles.

In the Introduction, I told you that soon after my mother-in-law died I had to go to the hospital emergency room with chest pains. My heart felt like it was going to pound out of my chest. I was nauseated. My hands were kind of clammy. My arms and legs were shivering. I was scared to death, sure that I was having a heart attack. Plus, my mother died of a heart attack when she was only 50, so I had the family heart history to worry about, to boot.

At the ER they started out treating me like a heart patient, but test after test came back negative (thank God), and in the end it was determined that my heart is healthy, and all of my symptoms were stress-related. The cardiologist told me, in no uncertain terms, to get a plan to manage the stress in my life.

That was the start of my own education about stress. Each of us has our own way of responding to stress, and we need to study ourselves a bit to figure how to change things:

- **Our personality plays a part:** People who constantly push themselves, or are especially assertive and aggressive may be more likely to develop stress-related problems.
- **Our career plays a part:** High-powered jobs like caregiving, medical personnel and public safety personnel are of course more likely than others to involve stressful situations.
- **Our family history plays a part:** If mental illness has shown up in your family, you are more prone to stress-related problems.

By observing how you react and respond to particular stressors in your life, you can create your own personal early-warning system. You'll start to recognize the mental and physical red flags that let you know it's time to put on the brakes and do what you can to relieve the stress you're feeling – *before* it overwhelms you and turns into a major problem. The earlier you catch it, the easier it is to fix.

What does stress do to me?

Stress is one of those built-in human responses that takes us back and connects us with our most basic and primitive animal instincts. I'm talking about the Fight or Flight responses in our bodies. If you were out in the woods and a wolf approached you, baring its teeth, would you stay and fight it off, or would you run away? When we feel stress, what we feel is our bodies ramping up to do one or the other, with everything we've got. Our amazing bodies were created to produce a super boost of energy in the face of danger, and to act at top levels. No batteries required.

When a stressful situation like that hits us head on, the brain sounds an alarm and sends out stress hormones like adrenaline, norepinephrine and cortisol. These hormones increase blood flow to the brain and muscles by as much as 400 percent! The heart beats faster. Breathing is faster (which brings more oxygen to the muscles and the brain). The muscles tense.

Digestion shuts down (so as not to take any needed energy away from the rest of the body).

In the modern world, there are some times that this fight or flight response can be very helpful. It's what's behind the stories you see on the news (I covered a few myself, actually) where a person was able to move heavy beams off of them and escape a burning building. Those powerful stress hormones were working at full power. The stress response is a wonderful thing during these moments. However, it's not every day – or even every lifetime – that we meet up with a wolf in the woods, or are trapped in a burning building.

The stressful situations we normally deal with may not be as dramatic or intense, but they are intense enough to call out those powerful stress hormones. If we don't have a wolf to fight, or a heavy beam to move, what are we going to do with all of that extra energy? If we don't find a way to manage it, or get rid of it, it'll swirl around inside us and do physical harm. Also, the more we activate those stress hormones, the harder it is for our brains to turn them off. So chronic, low-grade stress can have powerful negative effects, too.

There's no doubt that stress is related to illness. Recent studies show that 60 to 90 percent of illness is brought on by stress!

Some common stress-induced medical problems include:

- Migraines
- Ulcers
- Heartburn and Acid Reflux
- High blood pressure
- Heart disease
- Diabetes
- Asthma

- PMS
- Obesity
- Infertility
- Irritable Bowel Syndrome

Stress is also to blame for causing new, big health problems for people, because too many turn to cigarettes, drugs, alcohol or food for short-term fixes for relief. But that kind of "stress relief" can actually make the situation worse, because it doesn't touch the root cause and can actually leave a person more stressed out than they were to begin with.

What causes stress?

Change of any kind is a major cause of stress – the negative change related to losing a job, for example, but also the positive change that comes with a wedding.

In 1967, two psychiatrists, Thomas Holmes and Richard Rahe, came together to work on a project that would help others be able to figure out if the stressful events they were experiencing could cause health problems.

They interviewed 5,000 people who were being treated for some kind of medical issue. The doctors asked the patients to go through a list of different life events and check the ones that applied to them. Each life event was assigned a score (kind of a stress meter) and then the doctors developed a point system that would help to evaluate and estimate a person's health risks based on stress levels.

The Holmes and Rahe Stress Scale is still supported and used today. It's interesting that many, many caregiving-related issues show up on this scale. Want to get a handle on how your stress may impact your health? Check off the things that you've experienced within the past year. Then add up the points for each.

Death of a spouse	100
Divorce	73
Marital separation	65
Imprisonment	63
Death of a close family member	63
Personal injury or illness	53
Marriage	50
Dismissal from work	47
Marital reconciliation	45
Retirement	45
Change in health of family member	44
Pregnancy	40
Sexual difficulties	39
Gain a new family member	39
Business readjustment	39
Change in financial state	38
Change in frequency of arguments	35
Major home mortgage	32
Foreclosure of mortgage or loan	30
Change in responsibilities at work	29
Child leaving home	29
Trouble with in-laws	29
Outstanding personal achievement	28
Spouse starts or stops work	26
Begin or end school	26
Change in living conditions	25
Revision of personal habits	24
Trouble with boss	23
Change in working hours or conditions	20
Change in residence	20
Change in schools	20

Change in recreation	19
Change in church activities	19
Change in social activities	18
Minor mortgage or loan	17
Change in sleeping habits	16
Change in number of family reunions	15
Change in eating habits	15
Vacation	13
Christmas	12
Minor violation of law	11

Score of 300+: At risk of illness.

Score of 150-299: Risk of illness is moderate (reduced by 30% from the above risk).

Score of 150 or less: Only have a slight risk of illness.

Source: Thomas Holmes and Richard Rahe. Homes-Rahe Social Readjustment Rating Scale, Journal of Psychosomatic Research. Vol II, 1967.

It's important to point out here that not all stress is caused by things on the outside.

We can be pretty good at generating stress on our own, thank you very much. Things like worry, self-criticism, low self-esteem and pessimism are all common internal causes of stress. Also, note how many *good* things are on the list of stressors: marriage, vacation and retirement, for example. It's easy to forget this and then we wonder why we're so wiped out from something that was supposed to make us feel better.

How can I manage my stress?

It all comes down to training yourself to eliminate as many stressful situations as possible, and then creating a healthy plan for how to react to the stress that still does come your way – and it will. The goal, as I said earlier, is not to eliminate stress but to manage it.

We need to focus on learning how to relax so that stress doesn't cause us to lose joy and hope. We want to find balance and well-being. No one technique will work for everyone. No one technique will work for you every time. You need to experiment to find what makes you feel calm and centered.

This is important work. If you are feeling symptoms of stress, this is your opportunity to put on the brakes and make managing it a priority. By making time for yourself to practice stress relief, you are helping yourself to stay strong when dealing with life's challenges. *And all it costs me is ten minutes?* you ask. That's enough to get you started! What a bargain.

Let It Be

SO MANY WONDERFUL POETS have written about the idea that you simply can't change some things, so you need to accept them as they are. Honestly, being able to bring yourself to a place of such serene acceptance is probably not going to happen in ten minutes, *but* I included this concept here because there are some things that you definitely can do in just a few minutes that will help you to chip away at the hurt and anger you may feel when faced with an unchangeable situation. In ten minutes or less you can sit yourself down and:

- Make a list of three things you CAN control about how you react to the situation. (The ref made a bad call. What are you gonna do?)
- Try to think of one positive opportunity that could come out of the situation. Maybe a chance for some personal growth?
- Talk about it. Call someone who cares about you, and let them know how you're feeling. It won't change the situation, but hearing some understanding words can help you manage your feelings about the situation...or even gain a fresh perspective on it.

Take Care Tip #8

Activate Your Relaxation Response

THE RELAXATION RESPONSE IS THE exact opposite of the fight or flight response. I'm talking about an active mental process that you can learn, practice and train yourself to do anytime, anywhere. With it, you can trigger responses in your brain and body that will help bring you back into balance. Your breathing will become slower and deeper. Your heart rate will become slower. Your muscles will loosen up a bit. You're left with a relaxed body and focused brain.

There are several things you can do to achieve the relaxation response, including deep breathing (see Take Care Tip #3 in Chapter 1). And meditation. Now, a lot of you may think that meditation is an exotic practice involving chants and incense (maybe a little levitation too), but that's not what I mean here. Meditation is an ages-old way of quieting the noise of our busy minds and the outside world in order to experience the peace inside – a stressless, interior calm. Here's my recipe for meditation:

Find a quiet place – a garden, your bedroom, church. Get into a comfortable seated position. Pick something to focus on (either a single word or short phrase that you can say, or a special object that you can look at).

Then breathe. Find your focal point, and urge your mind to experience only the moment you're in. No worries about the past or the future. Connect with the stillness of the time and space around you in that particular minute.

When you first try this, it will take a lot of mental energy to keep your thoughts from wandering. But, the more you practice, the stronger your brain will become, and you will be able to realize deep, long-lasting calming benefits from your meditation time.

Take Care Tip #9

SELF-MASSAGE

RUBBING YOUR MUSCLES increases blood flow to them and helps to relieve muscle tension. It's a feel good way to boost your energy, too. Although a professional massage is most therapeutic, you can enjoy some of the same relaxing benefits with some simple techniques you can do at home.

- For sore shoulders: Stretch one arm across the front of your body, reach your opposite hand up and firmly rub the muscle above your shoulder blade. Switch sides and repeat. Finish with giving yourself a hug. Cross your arms in front and grab opposite shoulders. Squeeze and release a few times and feel the tension melt away.
- Stress can make it hard for us to digest our food. To help with digestion: After a meal, place your palm on your belly and slowly rub in a clockwise motion. That's the direction that food travels through your intestine. Help it along with this simple circular rub.
- For the feet: Put some golf balls in a plastic shoe box. Treat your feet by slipping off your shoes and placing them one at a time in the box, and rub them over the golf balls. This is a tip to share with the person you're caring for, as well.

Take Care Tip #10

MAKE TIME FOR TEA TIME

STUDIES CONTINUE TO SHOW that drinking hot tea can help your body and brain in many ways. Tea – especially black, green and red-bush tea – contains natural anti-oxidants that can help boost your immune system and metabolism, calm your brain, and even help your bone and skin quality.

Research is still being done to figure out exactly how much you need to drink to get the most benefits, but for now, many experts suggest two cups a day. For the healthiest cup, choose lower caffeine varieties (I like chamomile), and lay off the sugar.

Take Care Tip #11

BALANCE YOUR BRAIN

WHEN YOU'RE HAVING A TOUGH TIME figuring out a solution to a problem, you need to summon the super power of both sides of your brain. That's not easy to do when you're feeling stress. My friend, health psychologist Dr. Nancy Mramor, offers this little trick: Sit quietly, with your feet flat on the floor. Close your eyes, and take a few deep breaths in and out. Next, move your hands together and lightly bring the tips of your fingers together...try barely touching fingertips (eyes still closed). Feel the energy.

Dr. Mramor says this action works to balance your brain, bringing the strengths from left and right brain together to give you the mental blast you need to work your way through any trouble.

Prevent Tension Headaches

I KNOW A MAN NAMED TASSO SPANOS, who has the Center for Pain Treatment on Pittsburgh's South Side. He specializes in a practice called Trigger Point Myotherapy. He applies pressure to certain trigger points, and teaches people how to do light stretches that will focus on areas in a person's muscles that are the source of pain.

Tasso tells me that the #1 reported pain is the tension headache. The muscles responsible for causing tension headache pain are actually in the back of our neck, down the shoulder blades, and across the upper back. If you placed a coat hanger with the hook at the base of your neck on your back, it would outline the muscles I'm talking about.

Tasso says to prevent tension headaches you need to keep those muscles relaxed. Here's an easy stretch to help you with that:

1. Bend your elbows and place your palms together, finger tips up, as in prayer position.
2. Keeping your palms together, and as much as possible, your elbows together, slowly push your hands and arms straight up over your head. At the top, separate your palms, stretch each hand out to each side and bring them around to meet in the middle again at chest level, in prayer position.

Repeat this technique for a few minutes daily, or as many times a week as possible, whenever you happen to think about it.

Work It Off

STRESS RELIEF IS ONE OF THE MANY BENEFITS of regular activity. There's a whole chapter on exercise in this book for you (Chapter 3), but the positive, healthy aspects spill out into several other chapters.

Exercise helps with stress relief because it triggers the release of feel-good chemicals in your brain (let's hear it for endorphins!). All it takes is a few minutes of activity to start to feel that happening. So, take a break and walk the dog. Chase the kids around the back yard. Grab some light weights (or water bottles, or soup cans) and do a little arm work. Jump on the bed. You're an adult now and no one can tell you not to.

It won't take long to feel that stress slip away.

Find Strength in Numbers

GOING IT ALONE IS NO FUN, especially when you're trying to navigate through a stressful situation. Don't allow everything to rest on your shoulders. Relieve some of the pressure by sharing some of the responsibility with other family members. Take a few minutes and call someone else in the family you feel comfortable with. Confide in them that you're having a difficult time coping with everything, and that you could really use some time for yourself. Ask them if they could come and stay with the person you're caring for even for just an hour or two. A change of scenery will do wonders for you, and by letting someone else in, you're creating a long-term support network. At first they might be surprised, since you've always seemed so on top of everything, but chances are very good that this person will say yes, and will continue to check up on you, without your even having to ask. It will be wonderful not to feel so alone.

Take Care Tip #15

YOU CAN CALM YOUR NERVES by interacting with pets. There's a whole practice around this idea called Pet Therapy. I know a woman who takes dogs into nursing homes and hospices, and gets great results. People smile and laugh when they're around the animals. Their faces light up. Pets provide us with unconditional love and acceptance. A UCLA study found that the people they surveyed who owned a dog needed much less medial care for stress-related issues than those who did not own a dog.

Think about the therapeutic benefit of this for the person you're caring for, too. Even those confined to a bed can experience calm by being able to glance over to watch a tank of colorful, swimming fish.

If you don't want to take on the responsibility of owning a pet, you can still get the therapeutic benefits by borrowing a neighbor's pet for a couple of hours (most dog owners would be happy to have someone else walk the dog every once in a while), or volunteering a little time at an animal shelter. Most will be delighted to have the extra help. This one's longer than ten minutes, I know, but oh so wonderful if you have the opportunity.

Take Care Tip #16

HAVE A TREAT

THIS REALLY IS ONE OF MY FAVORITE TIPS in the book. As healthy-living as I like to preach, I am a crazy, chocolate-loving freak show. Imagine my joy when the news first came out about the health benefits of chocolate! Was I dreaming? No! Chocolate, especially high quality dark chocolate, has the ability to relieve stress because of a chemical reaction that causes the brain to release those same happy brain hormones (endorphins again) that are released during exercise.

Sadly, this is not a prescription to eat a lot of chocolate. Just a small square does the trick. Thoroughly enjoy it by eating it like the French do: place it on your tongue, close your mouth, and let it melt there. Don't eat, read email or watch TV – be still and quiet for a moment. Just you and your wonderful piece of chocolate. I learned that fine chocolate eating method from Dr. Will Clower, author of *The Fat Fallacy* and *The French Don't Diet Plan.*

Take Care Tip #17

Tune it Out

LOAD SOME SOOTHING SONGS on your iPod, click to the soft music channel on your TV, or turn on the good old-fashioned radio (it has knobs and a dial, as I recall), and let the melodies work their magic. Music therapy is practiced everywhere and gets great results with autistic children, chronically and critically ill people, and victims of abuse. It can work for you, too. Research shows that music has therapeutic qualities related to stress relief and mood improvement. This is why spas and upscale restaurants have it piped in. They want to create a relaxing environment for their guests. Do the same for yourself.

Take Care Tip #18

CAREGIVERS ARE FORCED TO be expert multi-taskers. We get used to running around doing many things at once. If you stop for a minute and look around, you might realize that not everybody moves that way all the time. It's OK to slow down and focus on just one thing at a time. Trying to keep up at that pace is not healthy.

Take a few minutes to pare down your To Do list. Prioritize what's left and try to focus on crossing off one thing at a time.

While you're at it, allow yourself a couple of minutes to reflect on everything that you are accomplishing. All too often, the successes get lost in the midst of everything else there is to do. Don't let that happen. Stopping briefly to feel some pride in what you do will help you feel confident and balanced throughout the day.

Take Care Tip #19

YOU MIGHT NOT REMEMBER the last time you let loose with a really good laugh. Now would be a great time to try to get that back. Read a few pages from a funny book, watch a little bit of a funny TV show, or call a funny friend and tell her to give you her best stuff. You Tube is filled with thousands of videos that will have you howling (just be careful of falling into a You Tube black hole and losing the whole afternoon). Laughing, even just smiling, helps to reduce stress hormone levels. Let something funny take you away from your troubles for a bit and give you a quick burst of happy energy. Maybe it really is the best medicine.

You'd better not be smiling. Stop smiling! Stop it right now! Did that work? I nail my kids with that quite a bit. Thought it couldn't hurt to try. Sometimes a silly little joke is all it takes. Did you ever hear the story of the three holes in the ground?

Well, well, well...

Just Say No

THIS IS ONE OF THE HARDEST TIPS for me to follow.

"Can you have that presentation done by Thursday?" *"Yep!"* "Can you help me finish my project this afternoon?" *"Absolutely!"* "Can you bake 30 cupcakes for the class Halloween party on Tuesday?" *"Of course, no problem."*

Saying "No" is not one of my strengths. I like to help people. I want to help people. Too many of us do that at our own expense though, and that's not good. It's really the whole premise for this book: we allow the work that we do for others to take up so much of our time that we don't have any time left for ourselves. Running from one thing to the next with no downtime is extremely stressful. Sometimes I wonder if the running back and forth is harder than the actual tasks we have to do. We need to develop some personal limits and to stick to them. That means you're going to have to refuse some requests of your time. Take a few minutes and think about how you will respond when you are asked to do something that you don't have the time to do (or you just don't want to do – it's OK to feel this way sometimes).

Sometimes having a script is all you really need to get you through it. How about *"I'm sorry I just can't this time, I have a family commitment."* Or what about the plain old truth, *"I'm sorry, but I've been doing so much lately, Tuesday afternoon was a precious bit of time I carved out for myself, and I really have to stick to that."* Who could argue with that? You're not hurting anyone's feelings like this, and you're not shutting yourself off from providing help in the future; you're just being a good manager of your precious time.

At first, you might feel a little guilty – but see if you can just wait a moment before you give in. In that moment, think about how you would feel if a friend said "no" to you in this gentle way. You'd understand, wouldn't you? Be a friend to yourself.

three

Get Out There and Play

❦

WHEN YOU WERE LITTLE you didn't worry about creating an exercise program to stay fit. When you weren't in school, you woke up with the sunshine, ate breakfast, and then ran outside to play. Your mom could see you when she called you in for lunch, and then again for dinner, and you'd come in for good when the streetlights came on. You were doing what came naturally. You didn't think about how many calories you were burning playing kick ball, you were just having fun.

Your body still wants to move like that, and being fit is still just that easy. It's tough to remember that sometimes, because you're grown up and the world has changed. Now we won't walk down the street to say hello to a friend. We don't even have to speak; we can just email a *"Whassup?"* The more that machines move and our muscles don't, the more we're hurting our bodies by not allowing them to do what they were meant to do.

It's easy to fool ourselves into thinking that we have been more active than we actually have. *"Whew! What a busy day,"* we say. We *feel* drained, and we *are* drained – mentally, even emotionally – but physically we may not have done much of anything, at least not consistently. We wonder why our hips are sore, why our shoulders hurt, why we have headaches. We buy fancy adjustable supportive office chairs to make us more comfortable.

We bunch up pillows this way and that to make us more comfortable. You know what would make us more comfortable? Getting up off our butts and moving around! I think the key to making regular exercise a part of your life is to make it fun. Just like when you were a kid. Think of the tips I have for you in this chapter as strategies to get out there and play again. (Note: *If you haven't done much exercise in a while, please talk with your doctor about what is OK for you to do.*)

Scientists have spent years analyzing the mechanics of the human body, and exactly like a machine, our joints were created with motion in mind. When we don't move, we get rusty. We put on weight and this puts us at a higher risk for serious illnesses, including heart disease, diabetes, some cancers and asthma. As I discussed in Chapter 1, caregivers are already at an increased risk for these things, which is why we need to give special attention to making exercise a priority.

OK, fine. *"Let's start an exercise program"* is crazy talk to someone who's burning the candle at both ends. I get that...but listen, we're not training for the Olympics here; we're not waiting for *Sports Illustrated* to call about the next Swimsuit Edition. All we want to do is feel better and be healthier. You don't need flashing neon lights and glitter to announce that you are going to start (cymbal crash, please) An Exercise Program. Working out doesn't have to be flashy or overwhelming, or expensive. I want to make this easy for you.

Here's what a doctor I know says to his patients who feel they don't have enough time for exercise: "Give me 30 minutes a day." When they say they could never carve out that much time, he says, "Then give me three ten-minute chunks, or six five-minute chunks, or ten three-minute chunks, or thirty one-minute chunks!" What he's doing is helping people to break down that big 30-minute number into manageable pieces.

As much as we don't like to admit it, sometimes we just want to be told what to do. So at the risk of sounding bossy, in this chapter I'm going to tell you what to do. You're going to get little, manageable plans to follow that will soon have you looking forward to regular activity in your day. If you are caring for people who can join you, you might even want to exercise together. There's no need to do too much too fast and hurt yourself. Don't rush these tips. Take your time with them. Enjoy the way that moving your body feels. Allow yourself to appreciate your new strength.

C'mon, can ten minutes of exercise really help?

One ten-minute tip alone is not an exercise program, but one ten-minute tip will start you on your way – and the most important thing you can do is to get started. Ten minutes of activity is much better than no minutes of activity, and the benefits add up quickly.

What's so special about 10?

Working in a newsroom for all of those years, I did hundreds of reports on the latest, greatest results of studies on health and fitness. Even for someone like me, with experience sorting through statistics, I have to admit it was easy to get confused because of conflicting information. Just how much of what type of exercise is 100% without-a-doubt the best? Recent research consistently proves that there are benefits to short spurts of exercise. Ten seems to be the magic number:

- Psychologists at Northern Arizona University in Flagstaff found that ten minutes of exercise improved mood, increased energy and encouraged mental alertness and clarity. Interestingly, more than ten minutes didn't bring about any additional benefits related to mood.
- Researchers at the Pennington Biomedical Research Center at Louisiana State University found that ten minutes of activity a day can provide immediate benefits, especially with heart health for people who haven't been doing much exercise at all.

Here's why: Ten minutes is enough time to increase your heart rate, get your blood pumping and oxygen flowing through your body and your brain. Within ten minutes your brain will release endorphins, those chemicals that make you feel happier and calmer. Exercise works faster than any pill. And by working activity into your day in smaller chunks of time, you won't burn out. Let me give you a little tough love here: *"I'm too tired"* is not going to fly as an excuse to get you out of this. Chances are you are too tired because you are not getting enough exercise!

The payoff?

After just a few ten-minute sessions, you'll notice that you're not so creaky when you get up out of a chair. Keep it up and you'll start to feel firmer. Your clothes might get a little loose. Others will notice and give you compliments and that's going to help you to feel better about yourself. Get moving and you'll have more energy throughout your day. You'll feel good, which will make you want to make other healthy choices. What you can accomplish in ten minutes will most likely leave you wanting more.

Also, as you may know, getting physical can also help you get physical with your partner. The positive mental and physical benefits you will feel from regular exercise can help a great deal with intimacy. Hmmm.

But wait, there's more...much more

Exercise will boost your immune system, making you less susceptible to picking up every bug you may be exposed to going in and out of hospitals, or spending time in your daughter's preschool, for example. Regular activity will help control high blood pressure. Exercise also boosts good cholesterol and breaks down bad cholesterol to reduce the potential for plaque build-up in your arteries. Research has shown that exercise is *just as effective as medicine* in managing or preventing Type 2 diabetes. Being active will help to strengthen your lungs by moving oxygen and important nutrients to lung tissues.

Moving more during the day will also help you to have a deeper, more restful sleep at night. I give you more details about the importance of quality sleep (and tips for how to get it) in Chapter 5, but for right now, know that when you sleep better your body is going to be able to function better.

If this information seems a little basic to you, I want you to remember that there's a big difference between knowing something and doing something. Thinking about exercise doesn't burn nearly as many calories, help your heart, or make your muscles stronger.

Fall back on these next tips as your go-to plans for fast, easy fitness. Ten minutes will make a difference. Try it and see.

This is gonna be good.

Make a Date with Yourself

GIVE YOURSELF TEN MINUTES to look at your schedule for the week and block out at least ten minutes for you to be active each and every day. I do this on Sunday nights. Start by going over what's already in your routine, and see how you can change some of your passive time to active time. Can you walk somewhere instead of driving? Can you replace a coffee break with a walk up and down the stairs where you work?

Then look at the time that's left. When you find a ten-minute chunk of time you can repossess, lock it in – **in ink**, so there's no going back. When you give yourself ten minutes to hunt down and block out your ten-minute dates with activity, you'll see it *can* be done. Keep this appointment with yourself just as you would an appointment with anyone else.

Take Care Tip #22

Just Walk

AS YOU KNOW, one of the best things you can do to lose weight or feel more energized is to move more. One of the easiest ways to move is just to walk! It's safe, it's easy and it's *free*. My friend, fitness expert Leslie Sansone, is the creator of Walk at Home, the #1 in-home walking program in the world. It allows you to pop in a DVD and get a one-, two-, even five-mile walk in your home by following along with her and her walk team.

Millions of people have lost weight and added years to their lives with Leslie's workouts. I lost 18 pounds in six weeks with Leslie's DVD's after the birth of my fifth child. The flexibility of the program is what got me to try it. I didn't have to leave the house. I did many of the workouts in my pj's, with my toddlers moving right along with me! I could do as much or as little as I could fit into the chunks of time that I found for myself. It worked.

Here's a ten-minute walking workout from Leslie:

Walk slowly to warm up for one minute.

Pick up the pace a little bit for two minutes.

Get moving to a brisk pace for five minutes and pump those arms!

Gradually slow back down, but keep moving for two minutes.

If you are able to take this outside, then go for it! The fresh air and sunshine will do you good. If you need to stay inside, switch to a march, and you can work out in a very small area.

☛ *And if you're ready for more...*

When you get the ten-minute walk down, try to fit in two more during the day. They will be just as effective as one 30-minute walk. You can increase the intensity by walking with some one- or two-pound hand weights, or throw a little bit of jogging into your walk.

Take Care Tip #23

STAND AND STRETCH

FOR THOSE OF YOU WHO ACKNOWLEDGE that you're getting older (I have been 35 for five years now), you may notice your range of motion decreasing. Maybe you feel like a circus act trying to put your socks on or zip up your dress. As we get older, our circulation slows, our range of motion decreases and our muscles tighten. Simply taking a few minutes to stretch can put the brakes on all of that.

Stretching relieves muscle and mental tension, improves flexibility and coordination and increases circulation. Regular stretching will help prevent injuries and make it easier for you to do all of the things you need to do during your day. Stretching feels good, too. It's easy, yet energizing.

Do some neck rolls, twist your spine and reach to the side, bend down and touch your toes. Aim to get nice full extensions of your muscles.

No matter which muscles you focus on, do it safely by stretching slowly and smoothly – no bouncing or locking joints, as this only increases stress and muscle tightness. It's very important to keep breathing as you stretch. Nice deep breaths, in through the nose and out though the mouth, will help let go of tension and increase the range of your stretch.

You can easily fit a few minutes of stretching into most days, whether you're sitting, standing or lying down. Take advantage of a few minutes even before you get out of bed in the morning, and *ssstttrretcchh.*

Take Care Tip #24

Sound the Alarm

SET THE ALARM ON YOUR MICROWAVE, your cell phone or your computer to go off every hour or two. When you hear the alarm, get up and stretch, walk around a bit. Just do something to get your body moving. It's easy to lose track of time when you're caring for others, and that little alarm will help to alert you to stop and spend a few minutes on yourself.

Take Care Tip #25

IT DOESN'T DICE OR SLICE but it is a total body gym that you can fit in your pocket or purse! Have you ever used a Firming Band? It's a long, narrow, thin piece of latex that you can take with you as a secret metabolism booster to use anytime, anywhere. They're sometimes called Thera-Bands, or Resistance Bands.

In ten minutes or less you can work your whole body. For example, to work your arms, sit and anchor the band on the floor under your feet, then grab both sides and do bicep curls, keeping your elbows close to your sides and bending and raising them up, then slowly letting them back down – holding on to the band the whole time. Repeat.

You can work your chest by holding the firming band out in front of you, arms extended and shoulder-width apart. Holding onto the band, stretch your arms out to the side, then bring them back in, and repeat. You can adjust the tension by moving your hands closer together or farther apart. I have more Firming Band exercises for you at *www.TakeCareTips.com.*

Registered Nurse Atiya Abdelmalik creates healthy lifestyle programs in her role as Manager of the Western Region of Preventive Health Services for Highmark, Inc. She uses firming bands herself and encourages people to keep one in a desk drawer, purse or briefcase. Think of all the time you spend waiting in doctors' offices. You can sneak some fitness in by pulling out your firming band and doing a few easy moves. If you're so bold as to put down the magazine and break out the band for some stretches with people around, you'll be setting a nice example too. Abdelmalik says, "As caregivers we go, and go, and go until our bodies break down and then we wonder how did we get here, not realizing that we've been on the journey to this place for a long time. To reverse the trend, do something for yourself even when you're feeling great. Don't wait for a crisis."

Take Care Tip #26

Get Strong

STRENGTH TRAINING IS NOT ONLY for members of the NFL. Simply put, strength training is doing exercises that push your muscles to work harder, so they grow stronger. A ten-minute strength training workout will get your metabolism going and keep your body burning fat for up to 24 hours! Try to do three of these three-step strength training sessions every week:

Step 1: Do as many lunges as you can in one minute. To do a basic front lunge, stand with your hands on your hips. Step out with one leg, and bend that front knee down low. Keep your feet planted and your back straight. Concentrate on your posture and take care not to bend your front knee to the point that it extends past your toes to avoid straining the knee or hip. Good form is important here. *Your back should be perfectly perpendicular to the floor. The calf of your bent front leg should be too.* From this position, drop your pelvis straight down, then bring yourself straight back up and repeat. Switch your legs, check your posture and repeat the lunges with the other leg in front.

Step 2: Do as many squats as you can in one minute. To do a basic squat, stand straight, shoulders relaxed, arms at your sides, feet shoulder-width apart, knees slightly bent. Keeping your feet planted, push your bum out to the back and bend your knees like you're going to sit down in a low chair. You can rest your hands on your legs or clasp them straight out in front of you, whatever's most comfortable. Remember to breathe. Hold yourself in the squat for a couple of seconds, then come back up to the starting position. Repeat.

Step 3: Do as many standing push-ups as you can in one minute. To do a standing push-up, stand about three feet away from a wall, stretch your arms out to the front and place your palms on the wall at shoulder level, but a little wider than your shoulders. Keeping your feet planted, lean forward into the wall, letting your elbows bend out to the side, keeping your back straight. Move in to let your chest come close to the wall, but don't actually touch your chest to the wall. Then, press into your hands and arms and push yourself back up to a standing position. Repeat.

Rest for 30 seconds then repeat the three exercises. Rest again for 30 seconds and repeat the series one more time.

This is a more intense fitness tip, so remember to check with your doctor before trying it. Keep breathing through the moves and do only what you're comfortable with. You'll notice your strength increasing, and it'll feel great to add one more lunge or squat to your routine as you get stronger.

Take Care Tip #27

Try Some Tunes

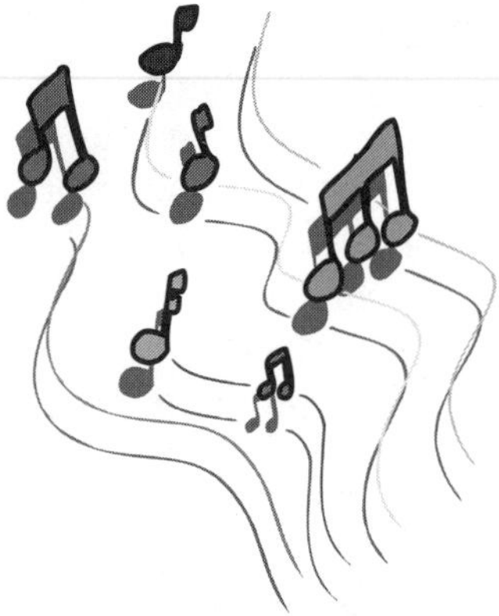

THE JURY'S STILL OUT ABOUT WHETHER listening to music can actually affect your breathing and heart rate, but plenty of studies show that people who have music going while they're exercising are happier, more energetic and feel better about the quality of their workout. The beat of the music helps to set your overall pace. Upbeat dance songs with consistent rhythms seem to work best. Lose yourself in some of your favorite music the next time you exercise and chances are you will feel motivated to work out longer and stronger.

If you don't just want background music, turn it up and dance for ten minutes! My kids and I have been known to do this at our house. You end up having so much fun, you forget that it counts as exercise. Think of all of the weight-loss stories to come out of that *Dancing with the Stars* show. Dancing works your whole body, and it's a nice cardio workout, too.

I go to a fitness class called Zumba, based on Latin dance rhythms. We samba, salsa and even belly dance our way through song after song. Teenagers and 80-year-olds are in the class. Everybody shakes it at his or her own level. Besides the fitness aspect, I love it because it's such a break from reality, and the time just flies. But remember, you don't need a class to let the music move you.

Take Care Tip #28

Give A Shout Out

CALL SOMEONE YOU ARE CLOSE WITH and tell them that you are now motivated to start taking better care of yourself. Tell this person exactly what you hope to accomplish, whether it's losing some weight or increasing your energy. In fact, make it a point to tell everyone you spend time with about your fitness goals.

You are creating your own support network. Maybe the people around you have been hoping they could reach out and help you in some way; they'll be happy to help to monitor your progress and keep you on track. It's easy to let social life fade away while you're caring for others. Creating this network is a way for you to keep in touch, and for you to get added support for continued success.

☛ *And if you're ready for more...*

Block out some extra time to actually go out with the people in your support network. See this as an opportunity for some healthy multi-tasking or just getting that important dose of friendship while getting fit. Run errands together. Do yard work or housework together. Sign up for a charity walk together. The activity and interaction are both wonderful for your wellbeing.

Take Care Tip #29

Get on the Ball

WHEN PATIENTS AT THE Physical Medicine and Rehabilitation Division at Allegheny General Hospital in Pittsburgh ask the Director, Dr. Barbara Swan, what the best exercise is, she always has the same answer: "The one you'll do." Dr. Swan helps many people with chronic pain. "I try to make them understand that if they're not healthy, they can't do anything good for anyone else."

She says you don't even need to find ten *extra* minutes if you sneak fitness into things you're already doing. For example, when sitting and talking, watching a TV show with or reading to a loved one, replace your chair with a fitness ball. You know, those big inflatable balls, sometimes called exercise balls or stability balls. They were originally used for rehabilitation, but their versatility and effectiveness make them a great tool for anyone to get a nice workout. If you've never tried a fitness ball before, you're in for a treat. It's fun. It's relaxing. You'll probably feel a little goofy the first time you're on it. You'll be a little wobbly – and that's why the fitness ball works so well. It forces you to use several different muscles at once to keep yourself balanced, so just sitting on the fitness ball and keeping yourself upright is a workout.

You'll strengthen your core muscles (all the muscles around your belly, front and back). When you have a strong core, your posture improves, your balance improves and lifting and carrying become easier.

Keep in mind that the harder the ball is, the tougher the exercises will be, so don't over-inflate the ball when you're starting out. Also, there are different sizes of fitness balls. Get the best one for you based on your height; check the guidelines on the packaging.

I sit on a fitness ball at my computer desk. My kids think I look like a giant chicken waiting for my egg to hatch. They laugh. So what? I'm happy to bring a smile to their faces, and guess what else? They line up to take turns to try it. Maybe this big chicken's not as loopy as she looks!

☛ *And if you're ready for more...*

There are hundreds of exercises you can do on a fitness ball to get all your muscles moving. Start by just playing around a little bit. Bounce on the ball to work the legs. As you move around, take the time to feel the different muscles that spring into action to keep you balanced.

Then try something a little more organized: From a sitting position, walk your feet forward. Lie back, and let the fitness ball support you. While comfortably lying on the ball with your feet flat on the floor about two feet away, stretch your arms out to the sides, then pull them into the center. Lower your arms back down to the sides, and repeat. You are doing an exercise called a chest fly and you can increase the intensity even more by holding light hand weights, or soup cans while you do the arm movements. Legs, abs, arms, and chest muscles all get some action with this exercise. (You can get more fitness ball exercises at www.TakeCareTips.com)

TALK THE WALK

I GOT THIS TIP FROM SOMEONE who was in the audience at a *Take Care* talk I gave at a women's conference. The woman is a caregiver to her husband who has Alzheimer's disease. This keeps her at home most of the time, so she keeps in touch with family or friend by setting times for weekly phone calls. She got the idea to use those phone calls as a way to remind her to move. When the phone rings, she gets up and walks around the house while she talks. She walks for the whole conversation and she even started wearing a pedometer to keep track of her movement. Two thousand steps equals about a mile, and the woman told me that she can sometimes get that in one conversation!

☛ *And if you're ready for more...*

Consider wearing a pedometer every day and keep track of your steps. Keep a little record of your daily numbers and make it a goal to increase your steps, even by a few, each day. Aim to reach 10,000 steps a day – that's five miles. If you need a boost, get into the habit of taking an extra lap around the grocery store when you're done shopping before you head to the check out. At work, walk a flight up or down to go to the restroom. Take your dog for a walk, or volunteer to take a neighbor's pet around the block.

four

Get in Here and Eat!

❦

LET'S CUT RIGHT TO THE CHASE HERE regarding the importance of nutrition, shall we?

More than 2000 years ago, Hippocrates, the ancient Greek physician (known as the father of medicine) said, "Let thy food be thy medicine, and medicine be thy food."

Not quite 2000 years ago, your mother (known as "Mom" or "Mama") backed that up, perhaps not as eloquently, with, "You're not leaving the table until you eat your vegetables!"

Not eating properly is one of the common fallouts from caregiving, and it's also one of the big reasons family caregivers are turning into patients themselves. Way too many family caregivers have poor dietary habits. I'm sure you know that food is your body's fuel. You need it to make you go. Not giving your body the fuel it needs – combined with stress and lack of sleep and exercise – is a recipe for illness.

If you were a car and you put bad fuel – or no fuel – in your tank, you'd just sputter along and then grind to a halt. It's very much like that with your body. So I'd like to take a moment now to talk about how the nutrients in food act in your body. You'll see right away why eating well should be a priority for everyone, and especially for caregivers.

What do I need to know?

Our amazing bodies can do a lot for us if we keep them filled with the basics so they can do their jobs. We have incredible high-tech systems built right in that can protect us from Alzheimer's disease, heart disease, many kinds of cancers and other illnesses. Medical researchers are finding that substances in foods actually have the power to give important orders to our genes – orders that relate to specific diseases.

For example, oleic acid in olive oil has been shown to *stop* an aggressive type of gene found in women with breast cancer. Nutrients in broccoli and cauliflower have been shown to *switch on* certain genes whose job it is to make us resistant to cancer in the digestive system. And all this is going on silently while you enjoy your olive oil and broccoli. Pretty cool!

Eating a variety of foods and drinking enough water boosts our immune system and increases our chances that our bodies will be able to prevent and cure any diseases that may threaten us – no pills required!

We've been hearing a lot lately about antioxidants in food. Check out the packages you have in your fridge; many probably boast *"antioxidants!"* on the label.

What the heck are antioxidants? They are substances found in fruits and vegetables, some vitamins and amino acids. They work to prevent and repair cell damage caused by the sun, smoking and aging, for example. And they don't stop there; antioxidants may also help to boost your immune system and decrease your risk of some cancers.

A nutritionist told me that the process works in the body sort of like how a piece of banana starts to brown after you cut it. Sprinkling on some lemon juice (containing Vitamin C, a powerful antioxidant) stops the browning/aging effect.

Lycopene is one of the most recent antioxidants to be discovered (scientists think there are probably many, many more still waiting to be studied).

Lycopene is what makes tomatoes (and grapefruits and watermelon) red. It may help to lower the risk of prostate cancer, breast cancer and cardiovascular disease, as well as a variety of other illnesses.

Bottom line: although many new scientific findings are opening our eyes to the infinitely complex ways that food supports the wondrous systems in our bodies, the old school lesson of balance, variety and moderation still holds true. That's the common-sense approach to thinking about nutrition.

So, what should I be eating?

In issuing its most recent report on dietary guidelines, the US Department of Agriculture stated that the "major causes of morbidity and mortality in the United States are related to poor diet and a sedentary lifestyle."

With the benefit of the latest medical research, we now know that we should be eating a variety of foods from basic groups including grains, fruits and vegetables, fats and dairy products. And we need to limit the amount of saturated and trans fats, cholesterol, added sugars, salt and alcohol in our diets.

Portion sizes are different for each of us. If you go to the Department of Agriculture's web site, *www.MyPyramid.gov*, you will get a customized food pyramid based on your age, sex, height, weight and level of activity. The food pyramid gives you the kinds and amounts of food right for you, along with recipe ideas for how to get the nutrients you need.

Eat for energy

Some substances in food can give us natural energy boosts, some substances in food can make us tired. Time to take a look at those.

If you're chronically tired, don't just assume that that always goes along with being a caregiver. There could be more going on. Now, it might be tricky to figure out if you're tired because you haven't eaten well, or you haven't had enough sleep, or because you have been under a lot of stress – or maybe because you are a little sick.

If you believe you are otherwise healthy and you're noticing that you just don't have as much energy as you'd like, start by analyzing and playing around a bit with when you eat, and how much you eat:

- Six mini-meals instead of three larger ones throughout the day may be what your body needs to run at its best levels.
- Check your portions. Regularly eating too much can lead to weight gain, which will slow you down. Not eating enough could deprive your body of needed nutrients. Women, especially, can feel tired if they have low iron.
- Are you eating too many empty carbohydrates, like white bread and sugary snacks? This can spike your blood sugar and then cause it to crash, taking your energy with it. Try to eat more complex carbs, like whole grains or fruit. Even better, combine them with with lean proteins, like tuna or cottage cheese, to stay energized longer.
- Are you drinking a lot of alcohol? It is a depressant.
- Are you drinking enough water? Dehydration can cause a lack of energy.
- Are you overweight? Extra weight is a big energy-zapper. Don't skip meals, but make sure to fill them with healthy foods, and get regular exercise (see Chapter 3).

Monitor what you're eating and drinking for a few days. If you feel like you're eating properly, but you still feel very tired, it would be good to visit your doctor to talk with her about your symptoms. Chronic fatigue can be a sign or symptom of many other things.

Eat for stress relief

Our bodies and minds are simply able to cope better when we're getting all of the nutrients we need. A lot of comfort food is notorious for its calorie and fat count, but has almost no nutritional value (and probably empty carbohydrates, too, so you crash after eating). There are plenty of things that you can eat to soothe your stress levels and boost your nutrition without adding the worry of weight gain to your troubles. Here are just some of them:

Berries: they're packed with vitamin C, which helps to keep the stress hormone cortisol at bay, and is a powerful antioxidant. Berries both help to protect your body and heal it from the negative effects of stress.

Nuts: it doesn't take a lot to do the trick. An ounce of walnuts, Brazil nuts, or almonds works to boost nutrients that can help to fight stress-related cell damage in the body. Nuts are a good source of protein and heart-healthy fats, too. Almonds are also said to help lower blood pressure.

Avocados: loaded with B vitamins, potassium, and vitamin E. Avocados help to keep you calm by replenishing these important nutrients to the brain and nerves. They're also a great source of – of course – avocado oil, one of the healthiest fats you can eat.

Oranges: your body doesn't make vitamin C by itself, and since stress can tear down our body's storage of vitamin C, we need to re-stock often. Vitamin C helps to strengthen our immune system.

Tuna: full of Omega-3 fatty acids, which help to regulate the hormone adrenaline (this works to give you fast energy boosts when needed). Choose white tuna packed in water for a low-fat way to enjoy the health benefits.

Spinach: contains high levels of the mineral magnesium, which helps the body and brain with several functions, including the ability to keep you naturally calm.

I'll drink to that!

As long as it's water, drink up! Two-thirds of our body is made up of water. It helps to regulate body temperature, promote good digestion, protect our joints and power our energy levels.

Water is so critical to the body that if you aren't putting enough in, your body will start to divert all of its energy to resolving that issue, instead of working for you in all the other ways it can.

There's a lot of talk about exactly how much water we need. The best answer to that question is probably that everyone needs a different amount. A 2004 Institute of Medicine report concluded that, generally, women need 11 cups of water a day and men need 16.

Keep in mind that some of the water (about 20%) can come from the foods you eat. The rest needs to come from what you drink. It's important to have extra water during exercise, as well as when taking some medications, or if you're on a high-fiber diet. Most importantly: don't wait until you're thirsty to replenish your H_2O.

Food and Family

I don't want all this nuts and bolts talk about your need for healthy food to take away from the simple fact that eating a meal together as a family can be a wonderful emotional experience. This can help strengthen your spirit.

My friend Pasquale Vericella is a husband, a father, a chef to the stars, and the proud owner of his dream-come-true: Il Cielo, a restaurant voted The Most Romantic in Beverly Hills.

To him, the restaurant represents the culmination of years of experience of his family's love of food and entertaining. To celebrate his successful 22 years there, Pasquale and his family started a program called R.U.S.H. (Restaurants United to Serve the Homeless) that he hopes will reach and help people in every city in the country.

Pasquale grew up around a mother and grandma who worked magic in the family kitchen with what they grew in their garden. "I can't say enough about preparing meals with family and eating together," Pasquale told me. "The lasting impression of learning how to cook from your parents, remembering the scent of the kitchen and the family's special recipes, the stories they told about how their parents taught them to cook, and the funny things that they experienced – it goes on and on. And then one day, you become the grandparent. We live with our memories. Life is a gift, full of shared love and experiences that we hand down from generation to generation."

Pasquale's mother died of Alzheimer's disease in 2000. His parents had moved in with his brother's family when it became clear that she needed 24-hour care. During his mother's long decline, Pasquale and his family flew home several times to spend time with her – and with his father. "We cared for them with love and enjoyed every minute of her last days. Stress, sorrow, regret, anger – all of these feelings came with this disease called Alzheimer's," Pasquale told me. "The only way to cope with all of that is to realize you must stay healthy and love yourself the way your mother (in this case) loved you."

As a person who believes that sharing good food can be a tangible expression of caring, Pasquale offers some from-the-heart advice. He believes that having a simple meal is a wonderful thing for a caregiver and the person they are caring for to enjoy together, because it turns into much more than a meal. "It's about sharing the normal experience of life with a person you are caring for," Pasquale says. "Making them feel relevant and, with Alzheimer's, helping them to remember the good times, the normal times. Enjoy every little smile, give them hugs, touch their hand. And don't forget to be funny! Eating together is an important part of caregiving."

Look for a few delicious, *fast* recipes from Pasquale in the Tips section of this chapter.

OK, I'm convinced...how do I start?

With Breakfast!

Boy, that's an easy meal to skip, isn't it? However, research continues to support that eating breakfast helps keep your mind sharp, your weight in check and your energy levels up.

A dietician I know suggests oatmeal with raisins, whole grain toast with peanut butter and an apple, or a toasted whole grain bagel topped with a slice of cheese. Quick and yummy.

Each of those choices includes a carbohydrate and a protein, which allows you to start the day with energy and endurance.

Here are some more ten-minute tips and recipes to help you keep your healthy nutrition habits going...all the way to the bedtime snack:

Easy Healthy Substitutions

WHEN IT COMES TO MAKING healthy changes in your diet, you don't need to worry about shopping for expensive, exotic ingredients or learning new recipes. Make it easy with just a few modifications to what you're already doing.

To eat more whole grains for example, use brown rice instead of white when you make stuffed peppers. Use whole wheat macaroni in your mac and cheese. Use whole grain bread crumbs in your meatloaf mix.

Ground turkey instead of ground beef for burgers and chili is another smart substitution. Top salads with flavored vinegar (balsamic or rice vinegar for example) and a splash of olive oil. For the salad itself, the more color the better! Choose a variety of dark, leafy greens, instead of iceberg.

Take Care Tip #32

COOK WITH SEASONAL, fresh foods whenever possible. They are less expensive, and many times faster to prepare. They are bursting with flavor so you don't need to spend a lot of time with seasonings. And speaking of seasonings, using fresh ingredients will help to keep your sodium intake in check.

For a fast vegetable dish:

Cut vegetables into chunks.

Marinate veggies in some light Italian salad dressing.

Grill until tender – works great on the BBQ, too.

Around here, we like to put zucchini slices and salad dressing in a big Ziplock baggie that we just pop in the fridge. When we're ready to grill, we dump the bag into a vegetable grilling skillet and in 20 to 25 minutes we're eating some delicious zucchini!

Take Care Tip #33

Fast, Fresh Broccoli

WISH YOU COULD HAVE SOMETHING tasty on hand for lunch that's actually good for you?

Here's an easy recipe from Chef Pasquale Vericella of Il Cielo restaurant:

Always keep a bottle of olive oil with freshly chopped herbs marinating inside it. (You may also want to add garlic, but it is *very important* to keep your garlic and oil refrigerated, and to use it within a week.)

Clean one head of broccoli.

Pour one tablespoon of the herbed olive oil over the head of broccoli.

Steam the broccoli until tender and then cut the stems off.

Place the seasoned broccoli pieces in a plastic zip lock bag and eat cool or warm for lunch.

☛ ***Bonus Tip!***

A can of white, albacore tuna goes great with broccoli. Enjoy a lunch with lots of vitamins and protein!

Take Care Tip #34

Have Some Fun (an Upside-Down Dinner)

ONE OF MY KIDS' FAVORITE DINNERS at our house is...breakfast! Dinnertime is when we make the things we don't often have time to make in the morning. For a speedy upside-down dinner, try pancakes or waffles. Add some fresh fruit and eggs or lean meat (turkey bacon for example) as a side dish, if you like, and you're all done. And here's where some of those substitutions will come in handy: instead of processed corn-syrup-based syrup, use real maple syrup. A little goes a long way. Or you can heat up some frozen berries and mix them with honey.

Yogurt, granola and fresh fruit make a great breakfast...or a dessert parfait at the end of the day. Anything will work, as long as it's fresh and healthy. Who said dinner has to be the same old thing?

Take Care Tip #35

EAT WELL, even on a busy day, by making the most of mini-meals. Some good examples of low-fuss ways to get your fuel include:

- light cream cheese and spreadable fruit (or fresh fruit slices) on a bagel half or rice cake
- apple slices with peanut butter or cheese chunks
- a mixed salad with beans and light dressing
- a cup of home-made soup (see Take Care Tip #39)

Take Care Tip #36

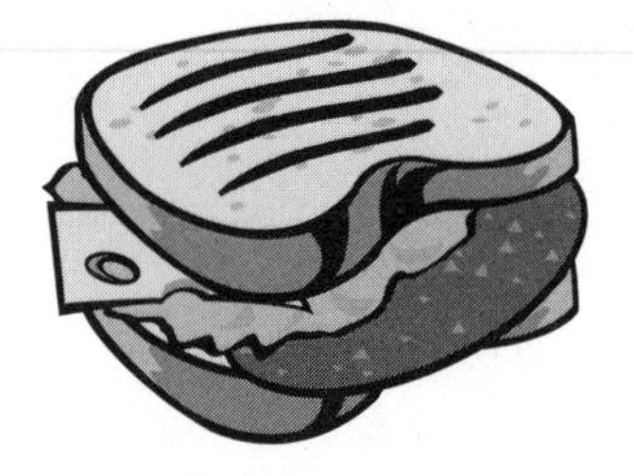

PASQUALE IS A GREAT BELIEVER in *pannini* – grilled sandwiches. You can put almost anything that tickles your fancy into your pannini.

Here's quick pannini idea from Chef Pasquale:

Buy fresh roasted turkey breast at a local market. Slice it down as needed.
Spread fresh pesto on the bread for added flavor.
Add tomatoes and slices of mozzarella, if available.
You can use any fresh vegetables and or leftovers, too.
Grill until toasted and warm. Let yourself be creative.

Pasquale says, *"The best sandwiches are never made the same way twice!"*

Take Care Tip #37

Easy Yogurt-Fruit Snack

IT'S SO EASY I hate to call it a recipe, but here it is:

Take 1 – 1½ cups of your favorite cut-up fruit (we like to use grapes, apples, pears, melons, strawberries or whole blueberries), and one small container (the kids' 6-pack size) of vanilla yogurt, or any other fruit flavors. Mix it together.

That's it – a fast, vitamin-packed snack that offers many more body benefits than the pre-mixed stuff.

Multi-Tasking Salsa

SALSA IS SO GOOD, so good for you, and so easy to make fresh in your kitchen. Once you do it yourself, you probably won't go back to buying it in a jar. The other great thing about salsa: you can use it for more than tortilla chips. I'll show you.

Jen's Favorite Homemade Salsa

1 large tomato

1 or 2 cloves of fresh garlic (I use one, but some of my garlic-loving friends use two)

1/4 of a large sweet onion

1 small bunch of fresh cilantro (I've always had good luck growing my own) a few squeezes of fresh lemon juice

I use a hand chopper and chop the garlic first. Then I add the onion and chop, and then the tomato and chop. I finish by adding the cilantro and the fresh lemon juice, and then I chop a little more. If you like, you can add a pinch of salt and pepper too.

You can serve it with baked tortilla chips and cut-up veggies. A word of warning: Make it right before you want to eat it. The longer it sits, the more the garlic flavoring comes out. If you know you will be storing it in the fridge for a while, definitely go with just one clove of garlic.

Your only job now is to decide where to use this multi-tasking salsa:

- Top toasted French baguette slices that have been brushed with olive oil (kind of a Mexican bruschetta).
- Use cold or hot as a sauce for pasta. Garnish with some reduced or low-fat cheddar cheese.
- Use as a topping for grilled chicken or fish – or your favorite egg dish.
- Use as a base for a pita sandwich. Add shredded low-fat cheddar cheese, some lettuce, and a little bit of reduced-fat sour cream.

Soup at the Ready

SOUP FREEZES WELL. You can ladle it into individual-sized plastic containers and reheat them whenever you want a healthy snack or quick, light lunch.

Chef Pasquale Vericella says...

"Buy chicken broth in quarts. Keep in the refrigerator. Quickly make a healthy chicken soup by adding your favorite vegetables. I like a head of escarole, celery, carrots, tomatoes and fresh parsley. Don't forget sea salt and cracked pepper."

Take Care Tip #40

FRESH HERBS CAN HELP YOU quickly and easily flavor your food (and give even store-bought dishes a fresh homemade taste). Many herbs will help to fill your kitchen with relaxing aromas too.

- Cilantro is great in rice, bean or vegetable dishes.
- Rosemary can be added to grilled chicken, fish or potatoes.
- Chopped basil is fantastic in pasta dishes and salads.
- Dill is wonderful in salad dressing or as a garnish for fish.

Take Care Tip #41

THESE ARE FAST, EASY and fun to make. They're packed with the nutrients you need for energy and endurance throughout your day. Kids love them too.

Simply toast a whole grain waffle.

Spread on some natural peanut butter.

Top with jam or banana slices.

Roll it up and enjoy!

Go Bright

LET YOURSELF GRAVITATE TOWARD bright colors when you're in the produce aisle. Brighter, deeper-colored fruits and vegetables don't just *look* prettier, they also have greater concentrations of important antioxidants, vitamins and minerals. The more color you can put on your food plate the better. It's a no-brainer way to dramatically increase your intake of important vitamins and minerals.

Take Care Tip #43

ANOTHER HEALTHY IDEA **from Chef Pasquale Vericella of Il Cielo:**

"Pack and keep healthy snacks with you for energy throughout the day.

My favorites:

Dried cranberries
Trail mix
Fresh fruit
Raw vegetables

I also make sure to drink lots of water."

☛ *Bonus Tip!*

To make it even easier to grab these snacks and go, package smaller portions in reusable snack-size bags or storage containers, so they're ready when you need them.

A Stress-busting Smoothie

HERE'S AN EASY-TO-MAKE TREAT that will help to calm your nerves:

Blend some low-fat milk, ice and a banana together and enjoy.

The banana and the milk boost the brain chemicals dopamine and serotonin, which help to regulate and reduce stress and anxiety. If you find that you need a little extra boost during the day, try adding some unsweetened protein powder to your shake for a snack or mini-meal.

five

Get to Bed

❦

DO YOU REMEMBER WHAT HEALTHY SLEEP IS? You might see people on TV doing it. They generally lie down in a comfortable bed, close their eyes, and stay that way for a nice, long while. It looks so peaceful. Why can't we do that? In this chapter, we'll focus on how you can get a good night's sleep.

According to statistics, it would probably be a great idea to start an overnight caregiver's club. The National Sleep Foundation reports that more than half of the adults in the United States experience sleep problems more than once a week. Two-thirds of the elderly people interviewed for the survey said they have frequent sleep problems. In fact, about 40,000,000 people in the US have diagnosed sleep disorders – and fewer than three percent of those people are being treated for it.

How did something so natural turn into such an issue?

What's the big deal?

Well, for those who don't have any trouble getting to sleep, it's hard to understand what could be the problem. But, for those of us who struggle just to let our bodies and brains enjoy a little rest, it's a huge deal! Often, the more we think about not being able to sleep, the more stressed we get, and the more we can't sleep. It's a bad cycle.

Plain and simple, humans need sleep. Sleep is essential to our health and well-being. It helps our brains recharge and recover from stress, and it repairs the cellular damage our bodies experience every single day. Most experts agree that somewhere between seven and nine hours of sleep is ideal for most of us. When we get less than six hours of sleep, we start to notice serious side effects related to our mood, our ability to function, and our body's ability to fend off disease.

This is something we all need to pay more attention to because lack of sleep can shorten our life span. Perhaps you remember hearing about a British study on lack of sleep released in 2007. For 17 years, researchers tracked sleep patterns and the health status of 10,000 government workers. The study found that people who regularly get five hours of sleep or less double their risk of dying of heart disease, and, due to their weakened, sleep-starved state, are at significantly higher risk of dying at a younger age from other diseases as well. In other studies, lack of sleep has been linked to an increased risk of diabetes, heart disease, obesity and cancers.

When we don't get enough sleep, we are at greater risk of other kinds of dangers too. The National Highway Traffic Safety Administration reports that drowsy or sleeping drivers cause at least 100,000 auto accidents every year (a conservative number, since it only reflects the reported incidents).

It's not surprising that chances of work-related accidents, mistakes and injuries go way up when employees haven't had enough sleep. In fact, some of the more tragic, history-making examples of on-the-job accidents have been traced to sleep-deprived night shift workers: the space shuttle Challenger disaster, the Three Mile Island nuclear accident, and the Alaskan *Exxon Valdez* oil spill, to name just a few.

But even if the physical health implications weren't so grave, we know from experience that when we don't get enough sleep it affects everything we do throughout the day. It's harder to learn new things quickly, we can't do our jobs as well, our stamina goes down, we lose energy and our memory gets fuzzy. When we're tired, we're grouchy, irritable, even angry. How can we provide loving care to someone when we're feeling like that? How can we provide critical loving care for *ourselves* when we're feeling like that?

As a caregiver, you may be managing and administering medications. You are responsible for your own health and safety, as well as the health and safety of the person you are caring for. This is a lot of important work to entrust to someone who's overtired. When we aren't able to get enough recovery time for our bodies and brains, we're setting ourselves up for the possibility of much more than a few yawns the next day.

Now, you may be thinking, *"Oh, I'm doing just fine on* [fill in with some number less than seven] *hours of sleep a night. I'm just wired like that!"* But listen to this: Dr. Daniel Shade, director of the Allegheny General Hospital Sleep Disorder Center, told me that our brains are able to adapt to lack of sleep, to the point that the effects of chronic sleep deprivation start to feel normal!

So, that makes it even more important to remember that even if you're feeling functional and fine, your body is just absolutely *not* able to function the way it should if you don't give yourself enough recovery between your demanding days. "When people are sleep-deprived, their performance level decreases," Dr. Shade says. "But there's a disconnect between how you think you're doing and how you're actually doing."

"It's sneaky," he added. "Like carbon monoxide poisoning."

What happens during sleep?

To look at a person sleeping, it doesn't seem like much at all is going on – but major repair work is happening. First of all, a growth hormone is released. That's why sleep is so important for children. But adults need that hormone too; it helps rebuild muscle tissue. Our brain is also very busy while we're snoozing. It sends signals that allow us to pass through the different important phases, or levels, of sleep:

We start with a light sleep, during which we can be easily awakened. As we continue to drift off, our brain activity slows down. We spend about half of our total sleep time in this floaty phase.

Next comes a deeper sleep, in which your body temperature drops and your muscles relax. This is when the immune system repairs any damage the body sustained during the day. In sleep studies, researchers use devices that pick up very slow brain waves – called *Delta waves* – during this time. There's no dreaming. Our minds are allowed to drift and let go of daily pressures. Our unconscious mind becomes more in control. Think of this as a deep, trance-like period of intense relaxation. This phase, by the way, is where infants spend most of their sleep time.

We actually go through two back-to-back phases of deep sleep, but suffice it to say, we're totally conked out for a while. If you woke up from these phases, you'd be pretty groggy.

After this comes the much-studied *Rapid-Eye-Movement* sleep, or *REM* sleep. In this phase, our breathing becomes faster and more shallow. Our eyes dart around quickly behind our eyelids. Our arms and legs experience temporary paralysis and our heart rate and blood pressure go up.

I didn't get this stuff from a horror flick; this is really what happens, and it's all very natural, normal and needed. REM sleep is when most of our emotional and mental restoration happens, and when we dream the most. Regarding dreams: Sleep researchers and some psychologists believe that these flights of imagination actually allow us to sort and clear out our thoughts, and then retain and organize the most important information we learned during our day.

It takes 90 to 120 minutes to go through all of these phases – and this is what is called the sleep cycle. To operate at our optimum level, we must go through the sleep cycle several times throughout the night.

With all this work to be done while we're sleeping, it's clear that if we don't get enough sleep, our brains and bodies *will* run, but definitely not at peak performance.

What's keeping us up at night?

Worry? Stress? Pain? A little bit of everything? Why, if it's so important, do we struggle to get to sleep… or stay that way?

As caregivers, we feel like we need to be "on" all the time. We have SO much to do, and it never feels like we have enough time to do it, so we get into the habit of staying up later and later to do just a few… more… things.

The next thing you know, it's two-thirty in the morning, and you have to be up for work at six. You collapse into bed, physically exhausted, but your brain won't stop (blasted brain!). You start to think about everything you have to do in the morning. What didn't you get done today? How are you going to fit it all in tomorrow? Great. Now it's a little after three a.m. and you've got less than three hours to bring your body back to a refreshed, renewed state. That's just not enough time for sleep to work its magic.

When you consider the extra stress that caregiving brings, it's normal that we would have an occasional rough night. Our bodies were designed to handle this from time to time. But if you start to find that it's difficult to fall asleep or stay asleep most nights, it's important to be evaluated for insomnia. There is nothing wrong (in fact it's very right) for you to call out for help if you need it in this area. Insomnia and other sleep disorders are more common than you might think, and there can be many different causes.

Insomnia 101: More women than men are diagnosed with insomnia, and older people are more prone to it than younger people. Major, prolonged stress can cause insomnia. Anything that changes or disrupts your sleep schedule (travel, or a different shift at work, for example) can cause it too. Your sleep troubles can continue even after the original cause goes away, because, as I mentioned earlier, your brain can seem to adapt to lack of sleep, and fool you into thinking you're doing just fine. It's easy for unhealthy sleep patterns to become a learned, accepted routine. Don't be fooled!

There are a variety of things that can keep us up at night. Here are some. Do any of them look familiar?

- Anxiety – deep, frequent feelings of worry, fear, helplessness and hopelessness.
- Stress – the pressure of coping with all the things in your life that require some kind of response from you.
- Depression – an all-too-common mental disorder that can make you feel very sad, tired and discouraged.
- Hormonal changes – whether it's PMS, pregnancy, or menopause, or everything in between, our hormones fluctuate constantly, and may affect our sleep.
- Age – as we get older, our *melatonin* levels decrease. Melatonin is a hormone that helps to promote and control sleep.
- Pain – muscle strains, stiff necks, and sore backs and joints are common sleep thieves.
- Your genes – some studies show that sleep problems may be linked to family history.
- Medications – many prescription and over-the-counter drugs can cause insomnia. Ask your doctor or pharmacist about the possible side effects of your medication. Speak up about any sleep problems

you may be having. Sometimes, it may simply be an issue of taking your medications at a different time of day... but talk to your doctor first before you make any changes to your medical treatment.

Don't fight nature!

All of the major systems in our bodies depend on rest and sleep to rebuild for the next day and start fresh. Before the invention of electricity, people went to bed when the sun went down and woke up when it came back up. Businesses also closed much earlier in the day. There was no overnight shift. We live much differently now. Changes in our culture have forced our bodies to change, and in some cases, to work against our powerful natural instincts.

When you think about it like that, it's easy to understand why your body reacts the way it does when you don't go to bed when you're tired, or allow yourself to wake up naturally when your body says it's time. You're interfering with your body's natural instincts, and your body's fighting back!

So what can we do?

The good news in all of this is that doctors who deal with sleep disorders are having great success with sleep treatments and therapies. Dr. Shade says that after just a few weeks of getting more consistent, quality sleep, patients say they feel like a new person. They are happier, more energetic, ambitious and satisfied with what they are able to accomplish.

That's where I want you to be. So, right off the bat, I want you to make sure that you're getting proper treatment for any underlying illnesses (cardiovascular disease and diabetes, for example) that can interfere with sleep. I also want you to tell your doctor or pharmacist about any over-the-counter or home-remedy type of medications you might be using to help you fall asleep. A number of pharmacies are equipped with a system that will automatically check any medication you take against your other prescriptions, to make sure they're compatible.

Next, try keeping a sleep diary. It can be a notebook that you keep by your bed. In the morning, date the top of the page, and then note the things leading up to or perhaps connected to the sleep you just had. Examples of what you might write in your sleep diary are: what you ate or drank before you want to bed, any specific stress-causing incident that happened, if you exercised that day, when you went to bed and when you woke up, how long it took you to fall asleep, how restful the sleep seemed, and if you woke up during the night. This will help both you and your doctor identify any trends, make a diagnosis, and recommend a treatment if needed.

There. That gets you started, now let me tuck you in with my ten-minute tips for how to achieve a good night's sleep.

Take Care Tip #45

Write It Off

ARE YOU HAVING TROUBLE falling asleep because your mind is like a huge to-do list? Get that stuff out of your brain. Keep a little note pad and pen on your nightstand so that you can quickly and easily jot those thoughts down when they pop into your head. It's simple, but it works. By writing the thought down, you can rest easier with a clear, relaxed mind, knowing you won't forget about it in the morning. You've given the problem to your note pad and you don't have to carry it around for a while.

Talk Yourself Down

ARE YOU TOO FRUSTRATED, maybe even too angry, to sleep? If you're mad because you're being stretched too thin, or because a loved one is sick, staying angry will make it very difficult to get a good night's sleep. Here's a deceptively easy positive-thinking technique that psychologists have used for years: Believe that you will feel however you tell yourself to feel. I know, this one sounds *too* easy, but you'll be surprised by your own power to talk yourself down.

Start by remembering that you don't have to lose the anger, you just have to put it to bed for a while so you can rest too. For example, if you're angry, think to yourself, *"I am really mad that I'm the only one running around taking care of Dad and that no one appreciates how much I do."* That's the anger part. Now here's where you take instant control of it. Think to yourself, "But I am choosing *right now* to feel calm, relaxed and secure." As you repeat this phrase over and over, try to breathe slowly and deeply.

Soon, you should feel calmer, more relaxed and secure. The anger will still be there if want to get back to it – you're not throwing it away – but this thought process gives you the power of control. With it, you'll feel like you're the one in charge of that emotion, not the other way around, and that feeling of power and security will help you to relax and fall asleep.

Doctors who use this kind of technique with their patients say that it helps to balance the body's energy and gives fast and long-lasting relief for insomnia.

Take Control of the Clock

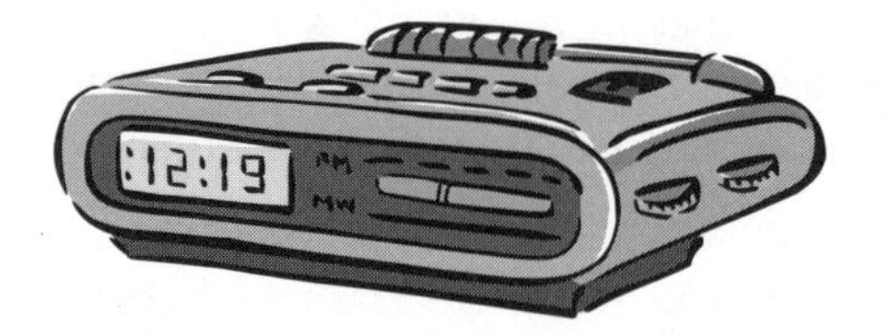

WORRYING ABOUT NOT BEING ABLE to fall asleep only makes it even harder to fall asleep. Practice the old "out of sight, out of mind" theory. Keep your alarm clock on the other side of the room, and turn it so you can't see the numbers. Tossing and turning, only to open your eyes to see 1:00... 2:00... 3:00... glowing in the darkness, will only make the situation worse.

Another way to keep the clock from ruling your night is to walk away. Sleep researches say that if you can't fall asleep within about 20 minutes or so of hitting the pillow, get out of bed and do something else. Move to a chair to do some light reading for example, or some journaling.

Move back to bed when you're ready. The idea here is to break any habit you might have to associate your bed with a sleep struggle. Many sleep therapists tell people to turn their bedrooms into spaces for sleep and sex – period. No reading or watching TV in bed. No catching up on work there, either.

Try to save your bed for only good things!

Have a Little Something

REMEMBER GRANDMA'S warm-milk sleep remedy? Well, there is some science behind it. *All* dairy foods are a good source of an amino acid called *tryptophan*. Our body converts tryptophan to the hormones *melatonin* and *serotonin*, which in turn have been linked to achieving quality sleep. (Other sources of tryptophan are oats, peanuts, bananas and poultry.)

If you want to try a bedtime snack that will help you nod off more easily (besides a glass of warm milk), eat a carbohydrate with a little bit of protein. This mix appears to be the best for increasing tryptophan levels in the brain. So, you could have a small bowl of oatmeal or cereal with milk, some crackers with peanut butter, or an apple and a piece of cheese, for example.

Now, just when I have you hungry, I need to point out that eating too much before you go to bed, especially too much protein, will work against you. Foods with a lot of protein also contain an amino acid called *tyrosine* that works to *stimulate* brain activity, which you don't want when you're trying to wind down. So, skip the leftover chicken wings!

Feel the Rhythm of the Night

EVER WONDER WHY WE turn off the lights to go to sleep? Forget about saving electricity for just a minute; I mean, do you ever wonder why we feel awake when it's bright and sunny, and sleepy when the only light we see comes from the moon and stars? It's because the cycle of light and dark, sunrise and sunset, all fit perfectly with a function in our bodies called the *circadian rhythm*. The circadian rhythm is governed by a pea-sized master switch deep within our brains called the *pineal gland*. Stay with me for a little more bio-speak, because this is interesting stuff: When the sun goes down, the darkness triggers our pineal gland to produce melatonin, which makes us feel like curling up in a nice soft bed and staying there for a while. When the light starts shining again, the pineal gland stops producing melatonin, and sends new hormonal messages to our body that tell us to wake up and jump into a new day.

This is the reason we get so wiped out when we switch to the night shift at work or when we travel and change time zones – we're going against our circadian rhythm.

Here's how we can get ourselves back into the rhythm of things:

First of all, step outside and enjoy the sunlight a little bit every day. When our pineal gland knows it's daytime, it will also figure out that nighttime will come when it's supposed to. The next thing we can do is make sure that it's truly dark during the night. This will tell your pineal gland, "OK, now produce melatonin!" If streetlights are shining through your window, pull down the blinds; if your nightlights could double as spotlights, swap them out for something that glows rather than glares. Most importantly, turn off the TV while you're trying to get to sleep. The combination of light from the screen and noise from those two a.m. *Law and Order* reruns will stimulate your brain, no matter how tired you feel, and work against your body's own natural rhythm.

Take Care Tip #50

Exercise for Sleep

SORRY, BUT I HAVE TO say it again: Exercise! Many studies show that regular exercise, especially cardio exercise – really, anything that gets your heart pumping – will help you achieve healthy, quality sleep.

It seems to encourage your body to move more easily between those sleep phases I told you about earlier. And when your body experiences focused, stimulating activity during the day, it will demand deeper, restorative sleep at night.

So, to improve the quality of your sleep, aim to raise that heart rate for 30 minutes a day, five to six times a week. As you know already, this will make a difference in quite a few areas of your life. Remember, too, that three ten-minute chunks of activity are just as effective as one thirty-minute lump. Those smaller exercise breaks will probably be a little easier for you to fit into your day.

A word of caution: Timing is everything. If you exercise too close to bedtime, your body might get too revved up to go to sleep easily. To give your body ample time to ease into the evening, try to fit your activity in before dinner, or take a walk soon afterwards.

Take Care Tip #51

IF YOU'RE A PARENT, you probably know about how important it is for children to have a consistent routine when it comes to bedtime. Well, it's just as good for adults.

Create a little bedtime routine for yourself. Even ten minutes of quiet time and deep breathing, brushing your hair, massaging your hands and feet, or some light, careful stretching is enough to make you feel comforted and relaxed. Turn down the lights and light a candle if you like (just be sure you're still awake to blow it out) – anything to slow the mind, and let the day go. Whatever your special routine, it will become a signal to your body that it's time to change modes.

The Good Night Wiggle

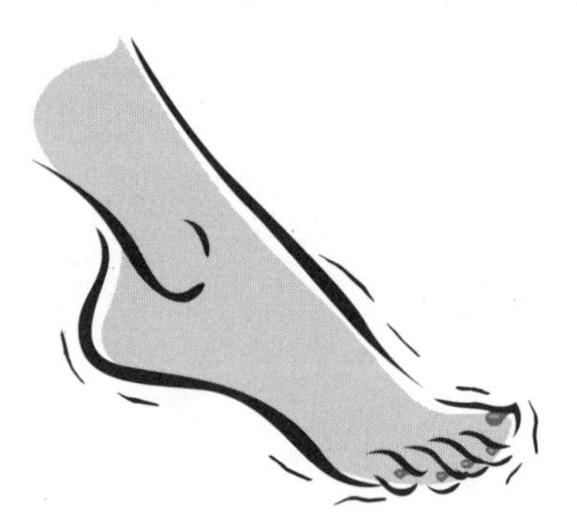

LET ME START BY ASSURING YOU that I am completely coherent. I am not on any medication. Here it is: If you want to get to sleep, try wiggling your toes. There, I said it, and I'm not sorry I did. I learned this from an acupuncturist who was a guest on my TV talk show. Apparently, lying flat on your back and wiggling all of your tootsies up and down for a little while will help relax your whole body and soothe your brain.

Toe-wiggling (for some reason it's even hard to type that with a straight face) is linked to the ancient science of Reflexology. This practice is based on the idea that everything in your body is connected, and that the different areas on your feet act like a kind of control panel for the rest of your body – your organs, your blood, your cells, your bones, your skin and your brain.

The action of wiggling your toes is thought to open up positive energy channels all through your body. With that kind of energy flowing easily through you, it's easier to rest and sleep.

☛ ***Bonus Tip!***

Wiggling your toes first thing in the morning before you get out of bed is said to jump-start that flow of energy and make you feel ready for your day. Seriously.

Ditch the Drinking

I'M NOT GOING TO CHARGE YOU a minute for this tip; in fact I'm going to save you time. I want you to stop fixing drinks that contain caffeine or alcohol before bedtime. Of course, it's good not to drink too much of *anything* close to bedtime, because you know what that will do in a few hours.

Alcohol and caffeine will interfere with your sleep in a different way. Some people say a glass of wine, beer, or a hot toddy helps them release tension and feel sleepy. That might be true – at first – but alcohol also interferes with your sleep cycle. A drink before bed makes your body struggle to drift into the deepest, most restorative sleep phases.

Caffeine, on the other hand, is a stimulant. It increases activity in your nervous system, which makes it harder to fall asleep. Lots of drinks, and even some over-the-counter pain medications, contain high amounts of caffeine. Check the label and switch to something caffeine-free.

Check Your Bedding

TAKE CARE OF YOU by keeping your space in bed as comfortable as possible. One study I found showed that 47% of people lose valuable sleep – that's up to three hours a week – because the person they're sleeping with is tossing and turning. Protect your territory! A bed that's big enough and stable enough will allow you to sleep the way you want to without feeling everything that's happening on the other side.

Maybe it's time to get a new bed. Take a few minutes to think about where you're sleeping. Ask yourself: Is it large enough for you both to stretch out and get comfortable? Do you wake up feeling sore? There are so many new kinds of mattresses and pillows now. If you haven't been bed shopping in a while, you may be surprised with how high-tech the industry has become. Companies do their own research to create products to address their customers' needs. If you're a side sleeper for example, you'll be able to find a mattress and a pillow that supports your style. Same for back and stomach sleepers.

Really look at your bedding, too. You work hard and you spend a big part of your life in bed. You deserve soft sheets, blankets, and comforters that wrap you up in comfort every night. There's nothing like high quality cotton and down – or even silk! – to make you feel like curling up and dreaming. Remember, quality sleep is not a luxury, it's a necessity every bit as important as good nutrition and physical activity to our overall health.

A Few More Important Thoughts about Sleep

Remember in Chapter 1 when I mentioned that caregivers are twice as likely to develop depression? Sometimes, not being able to sleep is a symptom of a bigger medical or emotional issue, like depression. Please, please, *please*, if you're having a lot of trouble sleeping and you think it's possible you're depressed, get to a doctor and talk about it. Depression is a medical issue like any other, and nothing to feel ashamed of ... or ignore.

And, if none of the tips in this chapter seem to make a difference in your quality of sleep, I suggest you talk to a doctor about the possibility of *sleep apnea*. People with sleep apnea experience shallow breathing, or even stop breathing, off and on during sleep. It can be caused by a collapsed airway. If you had this kind of sleep apnea, someone around you may have complained about your loud snoring (snoring doesn't always mean you've got sleep apnea, but it is one of the symptoms). Another, less common, form occurs when your brain sends the wrong signals to the muscles that control your breathing. About ten percent of the population has been diagnosed with the condition, but medical researchers think that many, many more people are walking around with undiagnosed sleep apnea.

A variety of effective treatments are available, but of course, those treatments can only be offered if there's a diagnosis.

six

Clean Yourself Up

❦

WHEN I'M OUT SPEAKING to groups, many of the caregivers I meet tell me that their daily beauty routine – if they're lucky – consists of brushing their teeth and splashing some water on their face. If they get to any makeup, it's whatever they can find in the bottom of their purse and apply in the rearview mirror at stoplights.

I know this. I understand this. So this chapter isn't about glamour girl advice. It's about understanding that how you feel about your appearance connects to larger issues of self-confidence and self-esteem. These things play a big part in your overall well-being. Putting ourselves last means that our appearance suffers too. You know that how you feel on the inside affects the way you look on the outside; the reverse is true as well. Walking around day after day in the same slouchy shirt and pants, hair becoming a rat's nest or hanging in our eyes, is just plain depressing – and that's not how I want you to feel.

Now, I'm not going to ask you to add "become eye candy" to your already long list of things to do, but I do want to help you realize that when you're *looking* rumpled and run-down, chances are good that you will be *feeling* rumpled and run-down. That doesn't help anyone – you, or the person you're caring for.

Mostly, I just want you to know that it's OK to care about what you see in the mirror, and I want to help you be happier about the person looking back at you. Sure, it's tough to think about making pampering a priority, with so many other "more important" things to take care of, but taking care of ourselves in this way is important too. A little attention to the outside can revitalize us on the inside. I believe that God gave us these amazing bodies with a charge to take care of them. When we treat our bodies with respect, we enjoy oh-so-many wonderful results:

Physically

Taking a nice bath isn't going to strengthen your heart the way a walk will, any more than brushing your hair will take the place of a few minutes with a firming band to help your triceps. But some time in the tub *can* help you to relax and keep your stress levels in check. And that's what we're after right now.

When you're relaxed, important physical things begin to happen. When you're relaxed, your body and brain don't sense any threats (that's basically what stress is – our animal reaction to threats), and your nervous system, heart rate, blood pressure and digestive systems all regulate to normal levels. C'mon! All that from a little bath? Yep! Or a shoulder massage, or a facial treatment, or a foot rub! – whatever it is that makes you think "mmmm...ahhhhh." They all trigger the same system-balancing physical responses in your body.

Emotionally

When you make time to slip away for a bath, manicure or massage, you send a clear message to others (and to you) that you are worth taking care of too. That's a nice reminder for everyone (including you) to have. And when you give some attention to your appearance, others will notice. If it just so happens that you get a few compliments for your efforts, then enjoy it! Those little affirming moments will fuel you, filling up your depleted tank with confidence and well-being.

Successful programs like Dress for Success realize this. They give women who've come through tough situations new clothes and coaching on appearance. And they've seen positive and powerful results: Their clients look better, feel better, and go on to get new jobs and start new lives. These women recognize that low self-esteem can make you miss opportunities because you're afraid to take them. If you don't have confidence in your worth, you won't speak up for yourself, and you won't have a chance at getting what you want.

Any act of caring for yourself is empowering and uplifting, and it sends a great message to your brain. Your brain can actually get in the habit of being depressed, but doing something just for you on a regular basis can help train your brain to be happy again. Take just a few minutes to make sure you leave the house projecting an image you are comfortable with (and that's key – this isn't about what those glossy style magazines say you should look like, but what feels right to you). Now you'll face your day in a more positive frame of mind, feeling competent and ready for any challenges that may come your way.

This self-care can also help to chip away at any feelings of resentment or anger you may have about your caregiving situation – the time it's taking, the energy it's draining, and that constant nagging question, *Why is it always me all the time?* Those feelings can creep in quietly and grow quickly. We don't always want to admit it, but it's common to become upset or even angry at the person (or people) we're caring for because of all the stress that's building up. A little self-pampering can go a long way to keep the internal peace by preventing those kinds of feelings from taking over. We each have our own special beauty and value – wouldn't it be nice to get in touch with that again? Think of the time you're spending on *you* as strength training for your self-esteem. A little bit, a few times a week, and soon you'll find that you're feeling pretty darned good. Count on it!

Your appearance matters to others, too

Kind of shallow, yes, but without a doubt, appearance matters in so many aspects of our culture. Several studies have shown that when people are perceived as pulled together and attractive they are usually treated with more attention and respect in a variety of settings and situations.

You've probably heard that we make judgments about the people we meet in as little as thirty seconds! Whew! That doesn't give us much time to make a good impression. I've also read that only about *seven percent* of what we communicate to one another is in words. The rest is all conveyed through our appearance, voice, expressions and body language. If this is so, then you can see how taking care of how you present yourself to others can greatly improve the way you interact with them.

If how we look weren't so linked to feeling good, and even achieving success, we Americans wouldn't be spending millions (billions) of dollars a year on lotions, potions, injections and implants to improve our appearance. But you know and I know that there's no miracle potion out there or instant glamour-in-a-syringe. Looking good is a *lot* simpler than that: It's about taking care of ourselves and then projecting that happy, confident feeling as we go through the world.

It starts when we're babies

We want approval. We want to fit in. We want people to like us. Behavioral science studies tell us that these issues are truly critical in our development. If these needs are not met in childhood, body image problems often follow us into adulthood.

A *Psychology Today* study (the 1997 Body Image Survey) showed that 56 percent of women and 43 percent of men who took part said they were unhappy with their appearance. A British survey of 3,500 women showed that two out of three women either have mixed feelings or feel depressed when they see themselves naked. (I hate to make light of this, but I can't help myself. I'd really like to meet the ONE out of those three women who feels happy about seeing her naked body, and then have a nice long conversation with her about how she does that. God bless her!) Seriously, these statistics are sad because if we are not happy with ourselves, it's tough to be happy with life.

Are you with me? Great! If you're ready to devote some time to taking care of your appearance, I want a commitment from you that you'll do what it takes to bring out the beautiful person that you are. You might feel a little guilty taking time away from other things that seem more important to focus on your appearance. This might feel a little dangerous, but let's go for it! Send out a media alert so everyone knows that you'll be out of the loop for ten minutes or so. Lock yourself in the bathroom and hang up a sign that says *KEEP OUT: Caregiver at Work.*

It's time to get excited and think of your pampering time as a little vacation from the stress you carry around every day. These ten-minute tips for appearance are your ticket to a happier brain and face.

Take Care Tip #55

SOFTEN UP

STRESS, DEHYDRATION, AND LACK OF SLEEP make our skin prone to dryness and roughness. Soften up with a homemade citrus-sugar scrub. In this quick and easy double-punch treatment, citric acid works to soften and loosen dry skin flakes, then the sugar scrub removes them, letting the healthy skin underneath shine through. Bonus Benefit: The citrus scent will give you a mood and energy boost!

What You Need

1 orange, lemon or small grapefruit

1/4 cup of sugar

1/4 cup of olive oil

How You Do It

1. Cut the orange, lemon or grapefruit in half, then squeeze *one half* of the fruit into a small bowl. Mix in 1/4 cup of sugar and 1/4 cup of olive oil (an incredible all-natural moisturizer – the ancient Romans used to slather each other with it all the time).

2. Take the other half of the fruit, and (trust me here) rub it over any rough, dry areas: elbows, kneels, heels, hands.

3. Now, rub the citrus-sugar mixture over those same spots. You can do your arms, legs, and shoulders, too – but do pay special attention to the rough areas.

4. Gently rinse, dry and enjoy your nicely scented, smooth, soft skin.

Take Care Tip #56

The Eyes Have It

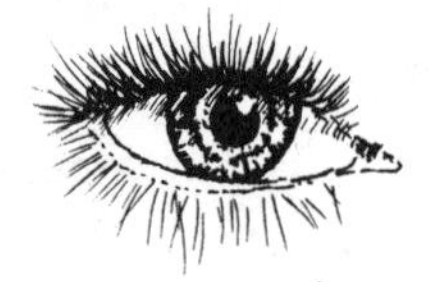

THEY SAY THE EYES are the windows to the soul. Eyes are the first thing we notice about someone's face. Keep your own eyes bright and lovely with these easy at-home remedies:

For Puffy Eyes

This one's an oldie, but it works: chilled cucumber slices. Either several thin slices or just one thick slice on each eye will soothe any puffiness. Cucumber is said to have anti-inflammatory properties and it goes to work in just a couple of minutes. Just close your eyes, lie back, place the cool cucumber slices over your eyes. Relax for ten minutes. Gently wipe off any residue with cool water, and then apply an eye cream or gentle, non-greasy moisturizer.

For Baggy Eyes

Produce to the rescue once again! This time, use raw potato slices over your eyes to tighten up loose skin. You'll see results in about ten minutes.

For Wrinkles Around the Eyes

More fun with food! Just whip one egg white in a bowl until soft peaks start to form. Dab the foam around your eyes, focusing on the skin at the outside corners and underneath, right down to your cheekbones. Let it dry, then remove, using a cool, wet washcloth or cotton ball. Kind of disgusting, yes, but my friend and makeup artist, Gina, swears by it (and she has beautiful eyes)!

To Brighten Eyes

In the palm of your hand, mix a little concealer with your eye cream and gently pat all around the eye to moisturize and brighten, together.

Take Care Tip #57

All Natural Beauty

YOU CAN CREATE home spa treatments that are every bit as wonderful as the ones you'd find at a resort – and I think they're even better, because you can customize your own aromatherapy products. Since ancient times, people have used essential oils from plants to help with a variety of issues: insomnia, stress, headaches and more. You'll find essential oils in everything from beauty products to natural cleaning products. There is some controversy about how effective these gifts from nature really are, but I know they seem to do the trick for me. They smell wonderful. Why not give it a try?

Here are a few suggestions for how you can mix up a potion just for you. You can get essential oils at the local health food store, farmers market or on the Internet (a little plug for me: I also sell them at *www.TakeCareTips.com*). Make sure you are buying 100% pure, therapeutic-quality essential oils. The man-made perfumed stuff isn't the same.

Start with two tablespoons of olive oil, then…

- Add 2-3 drops of lavender or tea tree essential oil and massage into your scalp to help with dryness and to stimulate the area for a healthy scalp. Tea tree oil is good for re-energizing your mind, and lavender can help you wind down. Leave on for ten minutes then rinse out.

- Add 2-3 drops of lavender essential oil and massage into cuticles, heels, elbows, knees ... any rough spots. The soothing scent will calm and relax you while you work on soothing that skin.

Breathe...

Add 3-5 drops of eucalyptus oil to a big bowl of hot water. Lower your head over the bowl and breathe in the menthol scent. You can drape a towel over your head and the bowl for a more intense experience. Eucalyptus oil can help open your pores as well as your breathing passages. This is good for colds too. Finish by wiping your face with a damp paper towel or washcloth.

Experiment!

You can sample oils while you're out shopping and see what makes you feel relaxed, tingly or happy. Add a few drops to your bathwater, or mix into olive oil and dab on to your temples and neck for a little aromatherapy-on-the-go. You can find a lot more aromatherapy ideas at *www.TakeCareTips.com*.

A word to the wise

Most essential oils you'll find in the store are safe for everyone, but please test these mixtures on yourself in a small area before using them all over. Full-strength oils (not mixed with olive oil or water) can sometimes irritate the skin, so it's best to mix them with a carrier oil (even olive oil from your pantry works just fine). Also, it is extremely important not to get any oil or residue in your eyes. It's always a good idea to keep your essential oils away from where any children in the house could get into them. Store your oils away from sunlight (which can diminish their potency) in dark glass bottles.

Take Care Tip #58

Plump It Up

FULL LIPS HELP MAKE you look healthier and younger. There are a bunch of expensive lip boosting products out there, but try these ideas before you buy any of them:

Mix a little bit of honey with sugar to create an exfoliating treatment that will soften dry lips and give them a healthy glow. Just massage on and tissue off. Your lips will be very sweet and kissable!

Another quick lip smoother: Rub some Vaseline over your lips and then lightly go over them with a toothbrush. Tissue off. Instant lovely lips.

The Multi-Tasking Bath

IT WOULD BE WONDERFUL to block out half a day for spa treatments, but that's probably not high up on your list of things to do right now. Still, you can give yourself five spa services at once while soaking in your own warm bath scented with lavender essential oil (see Take Care Tip # 57). Here's your multi-tasking plan while splashing around in the bath:

- Apply a deep conditioner to your hair and let it work its magic.
- Apply a facial mask that works for your skin type (how about the avocado mask in Take Care Tip #62?).

After you get out of the tub, while you're drying off...

- With one hand in your towel, push back the cuticles on your other hand. They'll be soft from your soak so it'll be quick and easy.
- Use a foot file to get rid of hard, dry skin on your heels.
- Finish with a rich body butter cream to lock in moisture, and help keep your skin soft and look pretty.

That's an awful lot of beauty in one bath!

Take Care Tip #60

Double Duty Products

YOU CAN SAVE TIME, SPACE AND MONEY if you cut down on the number of beauty products you keep around. You really don't need all the stuff the women at the department store insist you have to buy (sorry, women at the department store). Bronzers are a good example of a simple beauty product that can do a lot. A little goes a long way to add instant warmth to your face. When you apply it, think about where the sun would hit you, and sweep a little on your cheekbones, but also on the tip of your nose, and around the hairline. Bronzer works as an eye shadow and, mixed with a dab of lip balm or Vaseline, gives sheer color to your lips. Some cheek tints work as lip color and eye shadow too.

The point is, get down to basics. Set a timer for ten minutes and see how many old and unused makeup items you can throw away from your makeup drawer or bag. Only keep the things you reach for most of the time, and if it's time to update your look, keep your eyes open for some of these versatile products. Simplifying feels good!

Take Your Vitamins (and rub them on your face!)

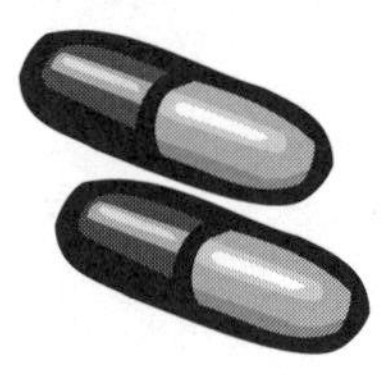

VITAMIN E IS AN ANTIOXIDANT that's said to protect skin cells from sun damage. It can help the skin look younger by reducing the appearance of little lines and wrinkles. But you can let expensive Vitamin E creams stay on the shelves. Most stores with a pharmacy sell Vitamin E capsules. Buy a bottle in any potency, use small scissors to snip off the end of a capsule, then squeeze the liquid into a bit of any moisturizer you have at home. You're getting pure, natural Vitamin E for your skin, and all you're giving up is the fancy packaging. Treat your Vitamin E the same way you treat your essential oils (Take Care Tip #57): keep it away from the sun and avoid using it full strength. As with sunscreens, you should apply your Vitamin E lotion about 20 minutes before going outside to give it a chance absorb into the skin.

Play With Your Food

BACK TO THE FRIDGE! Turn your food into a beauty-boosting mask. I'm about to ask you to do another pretty gross thing, but this tip gets results. We've talked before about how caregivers have a tendency to move through their day mildly dehydrated. When you neglect to quench all those cells that make up you, your body becomes sluggish and your skin looks dull. You know that an avocado has lots of vitamins and rich oils, right? So why not smear it all over your face? Yes, I did just say that. This make-it-yourself mask will instantly add moisture and nutrients to your skin.

What You Need

1 avocado, peeled, cut and mashed

1 teaspoon flaxseed oil (find it in the organics area of your grocery store)

1 teaspoon honey (any kind will do)

How You Do It

1. In a small bowl, mix all ingredients together until smooth.
2. Scoop it out with your fingers and spread it on your face, keeping clear of your eye area.
3. Try to relax (even though you have green goop all over your face) and avoid answering the door and frightening the UPS guy for ten minutes.
4. Rinse off with warm water, and enjoy your softer skin.

Take Care Tip #63

Be Handy

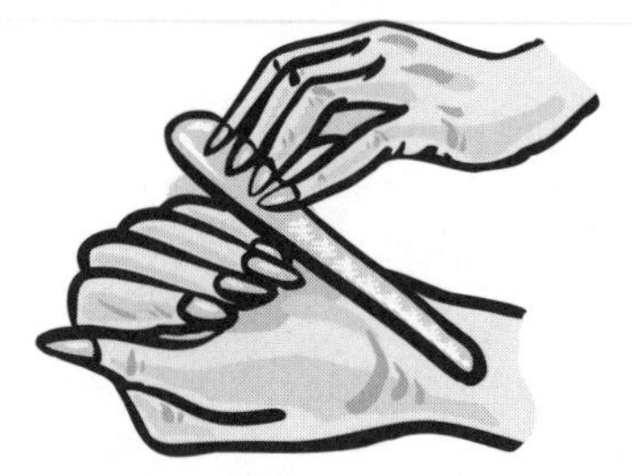

CAREGIVERS' HANDS AREN'T LIKELY TO be chosen for many hand-modeling jobs. Take a look at yours. Are they dry? Are your nails chipped? Cuticles cracked? Take care of those hands that do so much for others by spending a little time with a buffing block, which you can find in the beauty aisle of most stores. This is a little finishing tool that you that you can use to file, smooth out ridges, buff and shine your nails. The different sides go from coarse to fine, so you can do it all.

When you're done, treat yourself to a hand massage with a thick hand cream (preferably one with sunscreen, which will protect your hands from sun damage). I keep a buffing block and lotion in a basket on my bedside table so that I can sneak in a quickie mini-manicure every once in a while before I fall asleep.

When you do this, your nails will have a soft shine on their own, but if you want to go for nail polish, use a sheer, soft color that won't show mistakes or chips as easily. Flesh tones give a classic, well-groomed look, and go with everything.

Fast
Hair
Style

TAKE A MINUTE TO WORK a little bit of foam mousse into your hair at the roots after you shampoo. It will give you some volume, but the time-saving benefit comes from the alcohol in the mousse. It will help your hair to dry faster whether you blow it out or let it air dry.

Something Else to Think About

Ask your hairdresser for a cut and style that will showcase your hair's natural texture and drape. That sounds so common sense, but we don't do it! We kill our curls with flat irons, and those of us with straight hair use rollers or curling irons to build in some texture. It's just not necessary to waste all this time and energy. Stop fighting your hair. Ask your hairstylist to give you something you can style with your fingers. By keeping a simple, classic cut that works for you, you can cut down on drying and styling time, and save money on styling products and maintenance.

Now, if you're thinking, *"Don't worry about me spending too much time or money on my hair, Jen, I can't remember when I spent ANY time on my hair,"* this tip's for you too. A simple, classic style means your hair will fall into place when you want it to. No effort required, and you get a free boost to your self-esteem.

Take Care Tip #65

Have a Blast

MAKE THE MOST OF A TEN-MINUTE SHOWER by ending it with a blast of cool – even cold – water. A spa owner I know loves this tip. Warm water is relaxing to the body. It can lower blood pressure and increase blood flow and oxygen to the skin, which promotes tissue repair. *Cold* water makes the blood vessels under our skin constrict and then send blood to the organs, which helps with organ function. An invigorating cool blast of water at the end of a warm shower will instantly boost circulation, and make you feel fresh and toned. When you try this for the first time, I suggest going slowly: Step out of the water stream, turn the water to cold, and then kind of inch your way back into the stream (unless of course you don't care how many people you wake up with your shrieking). What we're talking about here is a home version of hydrotherapy, one of the oldest spa treatments in the world.

Lovely Lashes

WHETHER OR NOT YOU WEAR eye shadow or liner, a couple of coats of mascara will define your eyes, and add balance to your face as a whole. Before you use mascara, use an eyelash curler on clean lashes, which will help your eyes "pop." To avoid clumpy application, lightly wipe the mascara wand across a tissue before you use it. Also, try using mascara on your upper lashes only, which is quick and easy to do: Run the wand through your lashes in a zig-zag pattern to get a nice, even coating. Don't worry about the lower lashes. Mascara there can cast dark shadows underneath the eye.

EASY
TWEEZING

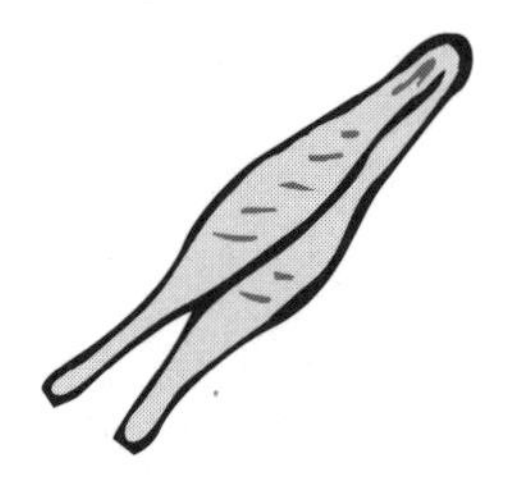

BEAUTIFULLY GROOMED EYEBROWS frame the eyes and make the face look great even when you don't wear makeup. Think Audrey Hepburn. Do not over-tweeze! Just spend a few minutes to clean up your natural line, and you will have an easy-to-maintain, polished look. You can sharpen your tweezers by rubbing some sandpaper on the inside tips. This will provide a good grip on those reluctant hairs and ensure a clean tweeze. If tweezing hurts you, you can numb your brow area with an ice cube or a little teething gel (just don't get any in your eye). Grasp the hair at the root and pull quickly to minimize discomfort. If you have sensitive skin that turns pink easily, work on your brows before you go to bed to let them recover during the night.

For extra definition, use a pencil or powder on a stiff brush and go over your eyebrows in short, subtle strokes, filling in bare spots if needed. Lightly go over your brow with a brow brush, or even a toothbrush, to blend. If you like, you can set your masterpiece with a touch of brow gel or clear mascara. Some models I know just slick a little bit of Vaseline over their finished brows to give them a soft shine. You may also want to try one-step colored eyebrow gel that comes in a mascara-like tube that you apply in one stroke.

The Brush Off

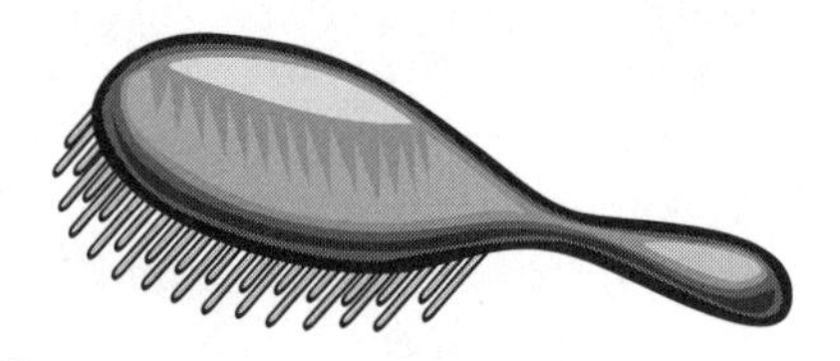

IT DOESN'T TAKE 100 STROKES a night to get smooth, shiny hair; in fact, too much brushing can take away natural oils and damage the hair. Just a few moments of brushing is all you need get the blood supply moving to your hair follicles, and to get rid of any dirt or dead skin cells. This keeps the scalp healthy and promotes hair growth. Gently brushing your hair is a good stress-reliever too. My hairdresser says you should only brush your hair when it's dry or almost dry, and make sure you get a brush that's right for your hair length and texture. For example, brushes with natural bristles are generally softer and less damaging, but they're not stiff enough to work on very thick or curly hair.

seven

Get That Mess Cleaned Up!

❦

IN A LOT OF WAYS, our homes are extensions of ourselves. They are our most personal environments. With this in mind, doesn't it make sense that your home should be your sanctuary, your retreat, your safe zone? It should not only provide physical shelter, but emotional shelter and support for you and your family, all of your habits, lovable quirks and individual needs.

But if your home is in a state of chaos, with stuff on every surface and closets like black holes, then your home is no longer doing its job for you. You don't have time to sort through piles of papers looking for the slip from the doctor that you brought home a month ago. You don't need to walk into your kitchen, take one look at the sink, and give a heavy sigh. Your days are crazy enough – why add to the stress?

When your home and your schedule are disorganized, your health and your overall quality of life suffer:

- When we're not able to find what we need, it causes stress *("Where the heck are my keys?!?").*
- When we're surrounded by things we don't need we feel unsettled, overwhelmed and out of control.

- It's hard to feel optimistic or motivated when your surroundings are cluttered.
- It's hard to think clearly with confusion all around you.
- Lots of clutter in high-traffic areas increases the risk of someone getting hurt.

You know that clutter in your home doesn't look good, feel good, or make life any easier. When you're trying to manage your own life as well as someone else's, you need to be organized and efficient to the extreme. It's really about taking control. Together, let's get control of your time and space. Let's try to fill each only with things that are helpful and healthy. Sound impossible right now? Stick with me...

Let's talk clutter

Have you ever watched those home makeover shows where a crew goes in and helps a family reclaim an area in their home simply by fork-lifting out all of the junk that's in it? I love them – not just for how pretty the rooms look afterward, but for how wonderful folks say they feel after going through the decluttering process.

When I watch, I pay special attention to the interviews the hosts do with the people about why and how their rooms got to be so messy in the first place. All the answers seem to have not only a time component, but an emotional one as well.

These people say they don't have time to create an organizational system for their home, and that it's hard for them to let go of a lot of the things that are cluttering up their space. Once the chaos has set in, they are totally overwhelmed and don't know where or how to begin.

You don't need to hire a fork-lift (though it might seem like that's the only thing that will help), but I do want you to begin just by looking around your space – perhaps the room you're in right now. As you go about your day, opening drawers and looking for stuff on your desk, pick a random thing up and ask yourself:

- Does this bring me joy?
- Do I actually use it?
- If it's old paperwork that needs to be filed, should it still be here?

Keeping and working around things that you don't need or want because you feel obligated to (it was a gift), or you just don't feel you have time to deal with it, drains your brain power, your time and your energy. And while it may seem daunting at first, getting rid of some of that clutter can change your life by replacing negative energy with positive energy. A clean space represents hope and possibility, and allows you to see clearly what you are able to accomplish.

To clear clutter and really make it last (and to make your home a warm and happy place), stop thinking in terms of throwing things away; rather, seek to use the things you have to their best, practical purposes. If you don't need them, you're not helping anyone by keeping them in your space. It will take a little time to create a system that works for you, because the process of living keeps potential clutter coming. There will be mail in the mailbox most days. The kids will get new toys. You'll get new clothes. You'll receive gifts. You'll take on new projects that have a lot of paperwork attached. But once you get that system in place, you will be able to welcome and manage all of it in a controlled, confident way – and you'll save a LOT of time.

Have you ever thought about how major life transitions are marked by parting with things from the past that we don't need now? Funny how that works. When a new baby is coming home, a space is cleared to welcome him; when you change jobs you clear out your desk; when you get married, you both get rid of enough stuff so you can – somehow – share a closet and a home; and at death, everything is cleared except only the most valuable to those left behind.

During each of these transitions, while the material changes are going on outside, emotional changes are going on inside. Remembering that you are creating emotional space as well as physical space makes these major transitions less stressful, and allows you room to contemplate exciting possibilities for the future.

On a lighter note, when you decide to invest the time you need to bring order to your home, you may feel like you've lost weight! And you don't have to cut any carbs. You are, quite literally, lightening the load and freeing your energy for the other things you want in your life. What a great feeling!

How did all this junk get here?

Even professional organizers have days and weeks when they are unorganized. Many things can bring clutter and chaos into your life, and caregiving is certainly one of them. Dropping everything to take care of a family member means that daily life maintenance often gets pushed down the priority list. If you're feeling sick, depressed or overworked, you might feel too tired to keep up with the housework. This is how kitchens seem to explode overnight. Throw in holidays, unexpected guests, extra projects at work, school functions and meetings, and your days are full of potential roadblocks to organization.

Professional organizers and psychologists (being so organized) have identified and categorized several reasons why clutter can build up. They include:

- Trauma – something important happens that causes you to drop everything else you were working on.

- Stress/Depression – you are so unhappy with your life that you can't see your way clear to do anything to improve it, so you give up.
- Perceived Lack of Time – you feel you are just too busy to devote any time to a big home project. You don't think you even have the time to figure out where to start.

My experience has been that clutter is kind of a slow, sneaky threat. And (this is not an easy thing to come to grips with) it's been found that the amount of clutter in your home is related to the amount of clutter in your brain.

A professional organizer friend of mine puts it this way: "Clutter represents unmade decisions." Thinking about that has actually made my stomach hurt as I've looked around at the stacks of papers on my kitchen desk (and table, and counter, if we're really being honest with each other here). Clutter represents unmade decisions – yep, makes me queasy. An overwhelming feeling sets in: *"How will I ever find the brain power I'll need to make all the decisions needed to get rid of that stack of paper?"* And, because it seems too intimidating, nothing gets done. But the stack of papers doesn't just sit there – it grows! Other people in the house start to think, *"This must be the place for papers."* So school forms get mixed in with mail, which gets mixed in with medical information, and it all starts looking really, really frightening.

If you know you have a clutter problem and you honestly can't imagine how you'll find the time or energy to fix it, just breathe for a sec. Then believe me when I say you CAN dig your way out, a little bit at a time.

As a family caregiver, there are many times where you feel that things are out of your control. This is one opportunity for you to have absolute control. Jump on it! The secret to being organized, for life, starts with taking time right now to make some decisions about how you're going to set up a system that works for you.

Organizing Basics

Starting with any room you choose, walk in and pretend that you're in a home that you've rented for vacation. What does the room look like? Does it seem like you could easily find everything you need? What does/ doesn't meet with your approval? Do you want your money back so that you can run someplace else?

When you realize you can't leave, because this is your home, think about the room in terms of efficiency first. Is it functional? Are you making the best use of the space?

Problem areas will stand out. Is there a pile of toys on the floor? A stack of mail on the counter? Those are the places that are screaming for some organizational help. Start with these easily identifiable areas, and decide on a fix that is easy to maintain. Taking care of those kinds of glaring trouble spots can be pretty quick and easy.

Work with them. You're not going for perfection here, but just getting a little more control of the space. For example, if that's where the kids always play with their toys, trying to move their whole play area could be a real pain. So let the space stay as-is for play, but corral those toys in a big bin or laundry basket so that they have a home other than the floor – and then establish a new family rule: Toys into the basket. Walk into any preschool. Those teachers run a tight ship! This kind of a system works there. It can work at home, too.

If your kitchen counter seems to be the most comfortable resting place for the mail, so be it, but place a basket or wooden tray on the counter to keep those letters and magazines contained.

Move around your home like that, staying focused on working with the obvious problems first. Yes, you are the one having to invest the time and energy to do the initial decision making, but once your systems are in place, everybody else in the house will know them and can use them. In the long run, this process will save you time.

Setting up an organization system also teaches the children in your house important life skills. It teaches them independence, because with all of their toys organized, kids will feel empowered around making decisions about their toys and other things as well. It teaches kids responsibility, because they are helping to care for the home by putting things where they belong. It teaches them to respect the value of things, because they are able to put them in a special place rather than just toss them on the floor. Perhaps you can even involve them in the process and see what ideas they have for a system – they will be more likely to use it if they feel like they helped create it.

Rome wasn't built in a day

If you have a lot of clutter clearing to do, thinking about all of it at once can make you nuts. Focus instead on keeping everything in perspective. You will feel better if you get your desk cleaned off, but the world won't end if it doesn't happen this minute. If an area seems too big to deal with, or requires too many decisions right now, go smaller. For those of you who look at that heap in the closet or the sky-high pile of papers and bills on the dining table (oh, I can relate!), and wonder how you'll ever make it go away, this is the key. You don't need to conquer it all at once.

You can start with just one Take Care Tip. Allow the results to sink in, and allow yourself some time to appreciate the progress you've made. Slow and steady will help you win this battle once and for all.

Take Care Tip #69

One Thing at a Time

ATTACK YOUR CLUTTER BY STARTING with the quick fixes: small spaces that are easy to spot. I'd like you to look around and think about what area in your home is bothering you the most. What causes you the most frustration ... trying to get ready for your day in a messy bathroom? Then spend your time there first. In a ten-minute chunk, whenever you can grab it, choose something there that you'd like to fix. Just one thing.

In ten minutes you can: clean off a vanity, move laundry to the washer, go through your makeup drawer, or ... (fill in the blank).

Take care of yourself first and don't get bogged down worrying about what you "should" do. Attacking the place that irritates you the most will help you the most. Keep this in mind no matter what organizing task you're working on.

Take Care Tip #70

Throw Ten Things Away

THIS TIP CAME TO ME from a woman who watches my TV show. She says when she finds herself with a bonus ten minutes (while dinner's cooking, for example) she walks around the house and finds ten things to get rid of. Sometimes it's a book or two to donate, sometimes it's junk mail to shred and recycle. She says her little ten-minute de-cluttering sessions help her to feel like she's accomplished something, and getting rid of even a few extras keeps her on the right track for her bigger organizing projects. You can throw stuff in the trash, recycle it (bonus points), or keep a plastic bin handy for things you want to give away (extra bonus points). When it's full, drop the contents off at your local charity on your way to work, and then bring the empty bin back home to collect more give-aways.

Take Care Tip #71

OVER THE COURSE OF OUR LIVES it's estimated that eight months are devoted to nothing but opening and dealing with junk mail. Every year the amount of junk mail sent out to homes equals more than 100 million trees! In response, forestry departments are planting more trees and communities are working with recycling companies to encourage environmental awareness programs. You can do your part too by reducing the amount of junk mail that comes into your home.

You can start by going to *www.DMAConsumers.org* and putting yourself on the Do Not Mail list. This is the website for the Mail Preference Service of the Direct Marketing Association; most companies that send out big volumes of mail refer to this list. Just fill out the online form.

You can get rid of most of those credit, mortgage and insurance offers by visiting *www.OptOutPreScreen.com*. This service is provided under the Fair Credit Reporting Act, which gives you the right to opt out of this kind of solicitation.

You will see a noticeable reduction in junk mail in your mailbox by doing those two fast, free things. Please note that it may take up to three months for you to be purged from all of the mailing cycles, so get the ball rolling now.

Take Care Tip #72

Clear Your Desk

DO YOU HAVE ONE OF those kitchen desks? My friend, lifestyle coach Mary Jo Rulnick, author of *The Frantic Woman's Guide to Feeding Family and Friends,* says that a kitchen desk can provide a nice, additional functional area in the heart of the home. But chances are that if you have one it's become a mini-junkyard filled with everything from the kids' craft supplies to the daily mail. If you've got a desk that doubles as the family dump, Mary Jo says you can make it useful again by clearing it off in little ten-minute projects:

- Organize smaller office supplies like paper clips and clamps, rubber bands, push pins and so forth in a small multi-drawer organizer. These organizers come in various sizes with any number of pull-out drawers, and you can find them at most office supply, discount, craft or hardware stores. Once you've put everything into its proper place, label each drawer with its designated contents so that everyone knows where to find and store stuff.
- Store larger and bulkier items, like note pads, stapler and staples, tape and ink pads, in a three-drawer cart with attached wheels, so you can move it around easily. Find one that can easily fit under your desk to utilize wasted space. School supplies like crayons, markers, colored pencils, paints and glue can go there too.
- Afraid smaller Post-It Notes with all those important jottings will get lost in the shuffle? A recipe box will keep them from getting lost. Staple the note to an index card, jot a key word at the top, and file.
- Have the kids go through their papers and art projects and separate them into piles. Scrapbook their favorites. Shred the colored ones to line a gift basket. Re-purpose artwork as wrapping paper or book covers.

Mission Control

TO MAKE GETTING OUT THE DOOR much easier for you and everyone else in the morning, set up a control center for frequently used items. Find a space to keep your checkbook, some stamps and envelopes, a pen and pencil, pair of scissors, neutral-colored thread and a needle (or a little sewing kit), change and a few bills (for lunch and milk money), any tickets or parking tokens your family might use, etc. You can use one of those multi-drawer organizers or anything that is easy to use and find stuff in.

I also recommend including a folder with all the important information you (or anyone else) may need related to the person you're taking care of. Make sure you put in a sheet with doctors' names and numbers, medications and any medical instructions. Having the essentials all in one place is a huge time and sanity saver.

Take Care Tip #74

Mark Your Boundaries

CLUTTER MANAGEMENT INVOLVES setting boundaries so that your schedule doesn't become cluttered as well. Think about things that zap your time on a regular basis and how you can put some tidy limits around them. One of the biggest schedule hogs is all this technology that was supposed to make everything easier. Nowadays we panic if we don't check our email every five minutes. I have a few friends who have created personal boundaries around email: NO EMAIL ON WEEKENDS or NO EMAIL AFTER 5 P.M. They stick to that and it has allowed them to reclaim some time for themselves; it's also made their computer time more efficient. Think of a personal policy you'd like to try, and tell the people you regularly correspond with what it is – chances are they'll think it's a great idea. If the BlackBerry is calling to you 24/7, try putting it in a drawer every once in a while – maybe during lunch, for example. Or set aside ten minutes every morning to clear out and file old email. Make your technology work for your schedule instead of overwhelming it.

Take Care Tip #75

Color Coded Closet

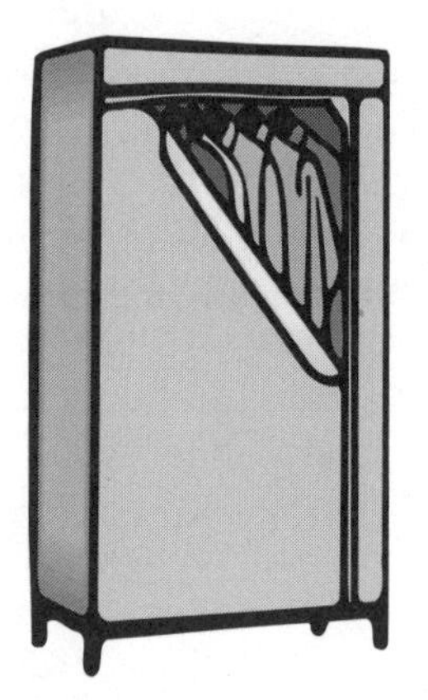

WHEN NEW YORK-BASED PERSONAL ORGANIZER and author Meryl Starr was a guest on my TV show, she motivated my viewers and me with her philosophy that finding happiness should be a priority. She showed us that clearing clutter in our lives can help us in our own pursuit of happiness. Her easy-to-use ideas for how to do this have been featured in dozens of magazines.

One of these ideas was the focus of our segment together: closet organization. Starr says after you go through your closet and you decide what things you want to keep, organize them by color, rather than type. So, instead of hanging all of the *skirts* together, hang all of the *blue* things together (whether that's a skirt, jacket or a pair of pants).

Starr says that opening up our closets to that rainbow of color is uplifting, and also extremely functional. We tend to look for outfits by color anyway, she said, so just work with that. It will be easier for you to see what you have and find what you want.

Take Care Tip #76

IF YOU'RE FEELING OVERWHELMED because you're reading this chapter thinking, *"I have more than a few extra pieces of paper hanging around!"* there's help for you too. If you have big bulky items you need to get rid of – worn furniture, for example – spend ten minutes Googling "junk removal" in your area. There are a bunch of national and local companies that specialize in big-time clutter clearing.

Most charge by the volume of the job (not the time it takes) and will provide a free evaluation and estimate of how much taking everything away will cost. If you decide to work with them, they'll schedule a time to come in a big truck (much less embarrassing than a fork-lift!) and move everything out. It's fast, and all loading and cleanup is usually included in the price. Many companies make an effort to donate or recycle the items that you no longer need or want.

Another option is to find companies in your area that will help you to sell your unwanted items online. They'll photograph your things, list them online, and arrange for delivery. Though they'll charge a commission for each sale, you'll get to clear out your space and make a little bit of extra money in the process.

MAKING
STORAGE
WORK
FOR YOU

IS IT A METAL BUCKET, or is it an art supply caddy? Is it an under-the-bed rolling storage box, or is it a game and puzzle cart that can be kept under the couch in the family room? It is what you make it! Customize your storage easily and inexpensively by re-purposing everyday items.

In selecting an efficient container, expert organizers say to look for something that:

- is sized to take up all the available space in the storage area so that you can maximize that prime piece of real estate. To fill a large space, use multiple stackable containers with lids.
- is see-through or allows you to clearly label it for fast finding.
- is sturdy enough to handle being bumped around and moved in and out as needed.

☛ *Bonus Tip!*

Remember to go through your storage containers for things that you don't regularly use at least once a year to make sure you still need everything that's in there. If you don't, let it go!

Keep a List

SOME PEOPLE LIKE DIAMONDS, others like fancy cars; I have always been drawn to pretty storage containers. There are so many cute ones available now. They tempt you (OK, me) to buy them before you even think about how you will use them, or if you even really need them at all. Bring all of these fabulous boxes and bins home, and soon the clutter in your home is made up of shiny, new storage containers with nothing in them!

Save time and money by keeping a *running list* of any new storage you actually need as you clean out your rooms. And remember, before you buy anything, see if you can reuse something you might already have for the same purpose (see Take Care Tip #77).

Live in the Moment

EVEN IF YOU COULD FIT INTO the size-6 bridesmaid's dress you wore to your sister's wedding, would you want to? Of course not. Then why is it still taking up space in your closet? If *"because it makes me think of how much skinnier I was then, and of all the fun our family had together on that day"* is the reason, well, it's time to donate it.

One of the harshest clutter-clearing gurus on the decorating shows I watch likes to remind people that things are not memories. Getting rid of the bridesmaid's dress won't stop you from thinking of that happy day – no matter how spectacularly poofy the sleeves are.

Keep the memories, but get rid of much of the stuff you have from the past, and you'll make room to live happily in the here and now. Sometimes it helps to have a friend come by to give you a little tough love during the cleaning process. If you can't bear to part with that purple dress with the huge shoulder pads, just because it was so expensive way back when, trust your friend when she directs it to the give-away pile.

☛ *Bonus Tip!*

If it's hard for you to part with some items, you could take pictures of them to keep in a little scrapbook, which will take up much less storage space.

Take Care Tip #80

Go Vertical

WHEN YOU NEED TO CREATE more storage area in a room, look at the walls. All of that empty space is available for inexpensive shelves that you can mount to hold books and containers. Hanging magazine racks help to keep reading material off of your table tops. I've even seen people hang wooden towel bars on the family room wall so they can store the blankets and throws they curl up with on the couch. You can install one shelf in ten minutes if you have the right tools: usually a pencil, measuring tape, screwdriver and maybe a cordless drill. No special skills needed. Keep your eyes open for all sorts of good-looking and cleverly designed shelf systems, rods or hooks, available in hardware and bed-and-bath departments.

Keep it Clean

WHEN YOUR HOME IS ORGANIZED, keeping it clean will be easier than ever before because everything will have a place. Once you've got some systems you like in place, I recommend a ten-minute clean-up at the end of every day, with everyone helping out. This is really all it should take to stay on top of the clutter.

Some Last Thoughts

To make sure you don't start to feel overwhelmed by all that stuff again, here are a few things to keep in mind as you go about your day:

- Analyze your shopping habits and make changes if necessary. Don't shop just to shop; always go out with a mission and a list.
- Don't buy something just because it's on sale. Nothing's a good deal if you didn't really want it to begin with.
- For every new item that you bring in, try to let something else go. If those shoes absolutely have your name on them, well then, there must be some old pair of sneakers in your closet that doesn't make you swoon so much anymore.

Each of these ideas reminds us to choose the things we have thoughtfully, with the goal of creating a productive and happy space in which to flourish.

eight

Why Don't You *Do* Something?

❦

THE TITLE OF THIS CHAPTER is taken from a great piece of Mom Psychology. Growing up, your mom never liked to see you just sitting around, right? "Why don't you *do* something?" she'd probably say. Once again, Mom was on to something: Just sitting around isn't good for us. Our brains need creative stimulation. Our bodies need physical stimulation.

It sounds paradoxical, but when we're busy and stressed out it's even more important to make time to do an activity just for the fun of it. Hobbies add color and excitement to life. I think one of the biggest challenges for many of us is to figure out how we can enjoy our own life while fulfilling our responsibilities to others. We might feel a little guilty even thinking about doing something light, free and fun. But I hereby give you permission to have fun, because lots of new research is showing that hobbies and other pleasant diversions are actually therapeutic.

Allowing yourself just a little break from financial worries, relationship issues and work pressures can be a wonderful thing. Don't worry – it'll all be there when you get back (sorry to say). Chances are, though, you'll be able to deal with all of it more efficiently after spending some time in a totally different, made-just-for-you world.

What's so great about hobbies?

It's simple: hobbies can bring happiness and joy to your life, and I want that for you. A few minutes with a hobby is an instant getaway from the tension and pressure of daily life. Doesn't that sound nice? Passive hobbies, like reading or listening to music, can bring pure mental and physical relaxation – and I'm all for that. But in this chapter I will focus on the more active, hands-on hobbies, like painting, beading or knitting. These will have those same calming benefits, but will also give you a feeling of accomplishment, satisfaction and pride as you put the final touches on your project or master a new skill.

There's a sense of wholeness and balance that comes with hobbies. Because you've taken time to get in touch with and express your creative side (whether it's making something yourself or losing yourself in a book or a song), you are nurturing your many dimensions, and giving yourself room to be a well-rounded person. Those kinds of feelings carry over into other parts of your life. You'll have more confidence and perform better at work and at home.

I would like you to adopt a hobby. I included this chapter in the book because I want to help you get back to you – and a hobby is a small way to do that. I'm going to lean on you a little bit to think hard about what YOU like to do. Some caregivers I've talked with don't even *know*. A small part of who they are slips away every day, to the point that when you ask them what they like to do, they can only laugh a little and say, *"Oh, it's been a while since I've done anything. I just don't know."*

That's so sad. You work hard to make things comfortable and happy for others – so let me ask: Is it OK to become so wrapped up in someone else's life that you lose the ability to find joy in your own? I didn't think so.

What would I even do?

C'mon, there's gotta be something you like to do. Maybe it's something you used to do when you were a child. Maybe it's something you've always wanted to do, but never took the time to try. Well, now's your chance. It's not too late. You can take piano or dance lessons whether you're 5 or 45 (or 85). I checked, and there's no law against it.

And guess what? I don't care, and neither should you, if you're good or bad at whatever it is that you enjoy doing. That's important. The great thing about being a grownup is that you get to be silly, exuberant, or even a little weird, and it's nobody's business if you are. A hobby is all about you, whether you're a latent Picasso or positively color-blind. You don't have to share your work with anyone, not even me (with the five kids, I don't have any more room on my refrigerator anyway). You're not doing this for a grade. I'll say it again: It's all about you. The only thing that matters is that you do it – whatever (and I do mean *whatever*) it is.

As you work on your hobby, you'll notice that positive feelings start to flow. The passion you feel for what you're doing will help to generate happier, more productive attitudes about things in general. Once you find and ignite that passion, you can feel secure knowing that it's there for you whenever you need it. Soon you'll find that spending just a few minutes on your hobby can lower your stress level dramatically.

Health Bonuses

A Swedish study, as well as research published in *The New England Journal of Medicine*, found that people who regularly spend even a little bit of time on hobbies that keep their brains active – things like sewing, gardening, or doing puzzles – are two-and-a-half times less likely to get Alzheimer's disease or other forms of dementia. A Japanese study of 12,000 people found that social hobbies can even boost immunity! It's also been shown that men with hobbies were less likely to die of stroke or circulatory disorders than those who did not have hobbies.

Certain types of hobbies have special benefits as well: knitting, crocheting, or anything that has you doing the same kinds of motions over and over, trigger that relaxation response we talked about in Chapter 2. This brings a feeling of peace, calm, and control. Your breathing actually slows down and your blood pressure lowers. Many studies have been done on hobbies as methods of stress-relief, and the findings are that yes, there is a definite connection. Some psychologists think that hobbies can even pull people out of deep anxiety disorders. Hobbies let us move beyond our worries; they allow us to temporarily transcend our doubts and fears by giving us a glimpse of our own potential.

There are proven therapeutic benefits of hobbies for the estimated 70 million people in the U.S. who have some form of arthritis. Activities like knitting, playing an instrument and gardening help with range of motion, and can significantly improve quality of life. Researchers at the University of Kansas found a lot of improvement in dexterity and hand and finger strength in patients with osteoarthritis who played the piano for twenty minutes, four times a week. (An interesting note: Studies also show that people with arthritis are more likely to experience depression, and we know that caregivers are also at risk for developing depression This is an example of how interlinked the issues affecting caregivers are ... as well as the remedies.)

Go with the flow

Psychologists also talk about the medical benefits of achieving something they refer to as *flow*, which represents the idea that there are certain activities in life that allow you to lose yourself in the moment. When you achieve flow, your body and brain are in a state of stress-free, positive, flowing energy.

Studies show that hobbies can lead to flow. For example, when you're playing a board game, the rules, objectives and goals are crystal clear. You can lose yourself in it. There's no need to think about what or how you need to do something (what a big difference from normal, daily life!). You roll the dice and move your playing piece. That's it. While you're playing the game, your brain is free to relax because it's not being called upon to sort through any intense issue. It's all pretty cut and dried: just roll the dice and move your piece.

What else can hobbies do for me?

Hobbies can develop your creativity. They will help you stay more focused. The concentration you achieve through your hobby will help to awaken your mind and boost your energy levels.

You'll walk through life a little bit differently, as a multi-faceted person, with more motivation. Yes, you are a caregiver, but having a hobby shows you also respect and develop your own unique, special talents, from yo-yo tricks to creative writing. Fostering that feeling of self-worth through an interest in a hobby will help bring you a new interest in life in general.

Many life coaches and corporate motivators talk about the power of taking a break from routine. Doing that helps you to develop new, different ways of thinking, which can help on the job with better presentations, faster problem solving, and more productive relationships with colleagues and clients.

Hobbies also make it easier for you to connect with others. There are quilting groups, photography groups, flower arranging groups, and so many more. If you find the time, you might be able to go out and practice your hobby – and meet new friends – in a local group of fellow enthusiasts. Even the most obscure hobbies have online community forums where you can talk to lots of people who like some of the same things you do, from all over the world.

As you think about what you might like to do, don't get too fixated on the idea that you wouldn't know where to begin. Most craft enthusiasts are eager to help an interested newcomer get started. You'll find that most of these hobby groups welcome "newbies" and will be happy to share tips, encouragement and interesting conversation along the way.

Cool Hobby Factoids

Some wonderful discoveries have come out of simple hobbies. For example, medical researcher Alexander Fleming discovered penicillin by accident when he noticed an unusual mold growing on some of the Petri dishes that he left out while he was experimenting with different cultures – this was his hobby (go figure), which eventually became his profession.

There may also be a connection between extremely smart, productive people and hobbies. A professor at Michigan State University found that among more than 100 Nobel Prize winners in the field of Chemistry, nearly all had a hobby of some kind, and more than half had at least one artistic hobby. I'll bet more than a few of those of those people are somewhat less than Nobel-level at their chosen pastimes.

Sounds good, but how can I possibly make time for a hobby?

Remember what I've told you about the health benefits of hobbies, and try to think about a hobby as a necessity. Tell yourself, *"This is not a fun break from reality; this is an important exercise that I simply must do to help me to be better at my other work."* That may help to get rid of any guilty feelings you may have about the time issue.

You can make spending time on your hobby feel like a priority by actually scheduling it in your planner. But don't get bogged down trying to find time that you can block out. Any little bit will do to get you started. It doesn't have to be smack dab in the middle of your busy day.

For example, one of the things I like to do is make scrapbooks. I find that the best time to do that is at night, after the kids are in bed. It's a very quiet, peaceful time in this normally busy house. I have some tea. I sit and look through family pictures, and it always brings a smile to my face (no matter what happened all the other hours of my day). It's so nice to end the day with a hobby that lets you go to bed feeling relaxed and happy.

If you need more structure, or more of a push to get you to try something, you could take ten minutes to find a class in your area. If you register and pay, you might feel more obligated to go and spend that time on yourself!

There are many ways that you can get the benefits of the hobby of your choice in small chunks of time throughout the day. Just find a way to get started. I'm hoping that you'll like your new hobby so much, you'll end up spending more than ten minutes every few days enjoying it. Here then are just some of the many stress-relieving hobbies perfectly suited for caregivers. If none of them tickles your fancy, get on the Internet or browse the *Hobbies* section of your local bookstore for more ideas.

GARDENING

SOME OF MY EARLIEST MEMORIES are of my parents and me in the big garden behind our house. I was a little girl who never really minded dirt or worms, and I still don't. Gardening gets you out to feel the warm sunshine and soak up some Vitamin D. It lets your lungs take in some wonderful fresh air. It gets you wonderfully covered in mud, if you're doing it with gusto. And growing beautiful plants from tiny seeds or cuttings gives you a huge sense of accomplishment.

Some of my most relaxing moments in the garden don't even involve the pretty part of the hobby. I find peace in just a few minutes of weeding or raking. It's active work that still allows you to daydream, and it feels great to see everything looking so nice when you're done.

There's science behind these happy feelings. There's a whole profession called Horticultural Therapy that is based on the spirit-soothing powers of working with plants. Horticultural therapists work to relieve stress among nursing home patients, the physically challenged, and prisoners. The artist Claude Monet used his garden to pull himself out of a deep depression. He then made paintings of it in the hopes of helping others to heal.

The benefits of gardening can come simply from planting and tending to a few basil seeds in a little pot on your windowsill, or arranging flowers in a vase on your kitchen table. You can also spend ten minutes poking around your back yard, making plans for what you'll grow next. Or you can tend to a container garden, which might be a more manageable way to get started. But whether your garden is big or tiny, most gardening activities – even things like watering, weeding, feeding and pruning – are pretty easy to break into ten-minute sessions.

PHOTOGRAPHY

IN TEN MINUTES YOU CAN CAPTURE more than words could ever say by snapping away at the world around you through your camera lens. Photography literally lets you zoom in and focus on the amazing details of life... or pan out and take in the whole wide world. There's a lot of hope in that. If you sometimes struggle to see the beauty around you, the camera can help you get back in touch with the color and light in your own world. You might find that you share that struggle with your loved one. Open their eyes through what yours are able to capture.

You can have fun setting up different themes for your photo shoots if you like. As you practice seeing and capturing life through a lens, you will begin to see things differently. Even a simple digital camera (where you can just delete the bad pictures...) can get you started, with no great skill required. But feel free to go as fancy or in-depth as you want. Keep a camera in your purse, pocket or glove compartment, so you can grab it and go if you're out and about with an extra ten minutes on your hands. It's as simple as aiming, then clicking the shutter.

Take Care Tip #84

JOURNALING

EXPLORING AND WRITING DOWN your own thoughts is a wonderful way to express things that you might feel, but are never able to say. Writing can help stimulate new ideas or calm your fears.

Journaling is an easy hobby to fit into your day. Keep a notebook handy so that when you find yourself sitting at a doctor's office, waiting to pick someone up from school, or by the side of a loved one who's resting or sleeping, you can jot down a few thoughts. If you're at the computer all day, consider taking ten minutes when you're done with your regular work to type any thoughts that have been swirling around your head. This is just for you – a nice way to end your workday.

It's also a perfect hobby you can share with the person you're caring for. This was one of the things that kept me going while I was caring for my mother-in-law, Me-maw, after her cancer diagnosis.

Her favorite color was blue. I bought a blue leather journal and we called it "her book." Late at night when I'd go back to her house after the late newscast, we'd sit together and I'd write. She told me so many interesting stories about her childhood and growing up with her brothers and sister in an orphanage.

I asked her about her husband and about each one of her children and grandchildren. What things she loved about each of them. What she hoped for each of them. Special times that she remembered sharing with each of them.

This hobby was for both of us. It was a way for her to share stories and feelings that she didn't want to be forgotten. It offered me a sense of control. Here was something concrete and positive that I could bring to the situation to make it a little bit better.

I left Me-ma's house the rainy night that she died, came home, and typed long excerpts from that little blue leather book into my computer. I burned the files and some pictures to a disc, took it to a 24-hour copy center and asked them to print me a dozen bound books.

I was able to give these to our family after the funeral mass. It was extremely rewarding to be able to offer something positive at that time, something that would help keep her spirit close.

You see, hobbies aren't just ways to pass the time, but tools for the spirit. You may want to try sharing a journal with someone, like I did, or you can just keep it to yourself. It is truly up to you to decide where your hobby belongs in your life.

PUZZLES

SEEMS LIKE THE ONLY TIME my family thinks to break out a puzzle is when we stumble across a few tucked in a closet some place we're staying on vacation. We find a space to set it up and it stays there until it's done. Sometimes it takes us all week to finish a big puzzle with lots of little pieces, but we chip away at it just a little bit at a time, and it all comes together. Sometimes just one of us works on it; another time, we work on it together.

Working on puzzles is a nice hobby because it's inexpensive. (You can find them for a quarter or two at yard sales – but beware those missing pieces!) It's also very quiet, so you can do it early in the morning or late at night, while people are sleeping.

Puzzles were part of that study I told you about earlier – one of the active-mind activities that will help to prevent all kinds of dementia. If you're feeling especially hungry for a brain challenge, find one of those intentionally difficult puzzles and have at it!

SCRAPBOOKING

WHILE JOURNALING ALLOWS YOU to tell a story through words, scrapbooking lets you tell it through pictures. You can tap into a lot of creative energy by working with your hands to clip, design and embellish.

Although I've seen (and made) very ornate scrapbooks, I know that it's easy to get lost or intimidated in the scrapbooking aisle. But really, you just need a few basic supplies to get started:

- Some photos
- A blank scrapbook
- A pair of scissors (to cut photos or paper as needed)
- Some acid-free paper (It's treated so it won't damage your photos. You can find it anywhere you buy craft supplies)
- An acid-free pen or thin marker (so that you can add a little bit of journaling or captions. These are sold in craft, office supply and photo stores)
- An acid-free glue stick or adhesive squares for attaching your photos to the pages (you'll find it right with the scrapbooking stuff)

You can do a lot in ten-minute chunks to advance your scrapbooking hobby: You can organize and select photos you'd like to use on a page. You can write some notes to go with the photos, or your journaling thoughts. You can go through your stash and choose what papers you'd like to use.

Then, when you have a little more time, you can have fun bringing all of the elements together to create a page. It's pretty hard to get bored with scrapbooking. There are always new products and techniques to try.

Now, as I said before, your hobby is yours; your scrapbook can be your own private collection of memories, or if you like, a gift for the family and a keepsake for all to enjoy.

Knitting, Crochet, and Needlework

NEEDLE ARTS GO BACK thousands of years, and just recently there's been a big resurgence in knitting, crocheting and needlework. People who know and love this hobby have raved about its health benefits for a long time, and now, people in the medical community are starting to agree.

The mind-calming, strengthening and balancing effects of knitting are said to be similar to the kinds of feelings you can achieve through yoga. A Harvard Medical School Mind/Body Institute report shows that when a person knits, their heart rate and blood pressure drop. Several organizations are paying attention to these findings and are now offering knitting classes and groups in cancer support centers, hospices, corporate health and wellness programs, senior citizens centers and even children's hospitals.

Learning the basics of knitting doesn't take a lot of time, and practicing is soothing. Several books and web sites offer knitting instructions. Many craft stores offer low-cost classes, too.

Take Care Tip #88

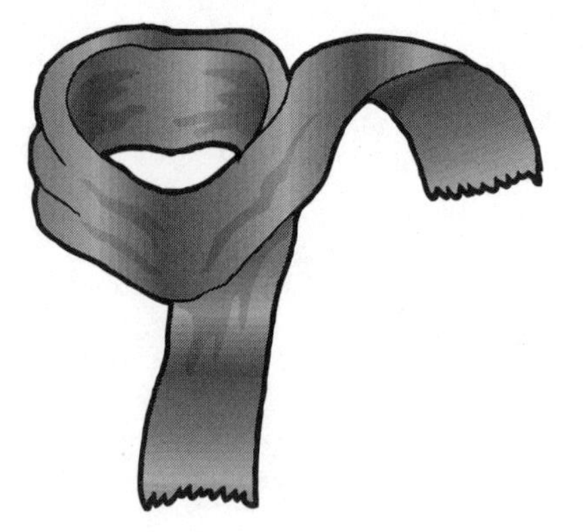

IF IT'S BEEN A WHILE SINCE you've tried any crafting, or if you don't consider yourself crafty at all, but you'd like to try something, I have two words for you: Polar Fleece. Just looking at the rainbow of available polar fleece colors all lined up on the shelves of the fabric store will bring a smile to your face. Polar fleece is soft and cuddly. It doesn't fray. It's criminally easy to work with.

Making a cozy scarf or a throw blanket is as simple as cutting a piece of polar fleece to the size you want. You can cut fringe around the edge to finish your project off.

You didn't skip over the rest of the directions. Cut and fringe. You're done!

I like to make reversible throws by cutting out two pieces of fleece in different colors. Place the pieces together, and make a four- or five-inch fringe all the way around, cutting through both pieces. Bring one piece of fringe in each color together and tie in a knot. Do that the whole way around.

These fast, easy, inexpensive projects make thoughtful gifts. Customize them by using your favorite team's colors (it's all Black and Gold here!), or school colors.

☛ *Bonus Tip!*

You can use this technique to update the pillows in your home for the seasons or holidays. Just cut two pieces of fleece to the size of the pillow you want to cover, with some extra length for the fringe. Cut the fringe, place one piece of fleece on either side of the pillow and tie away!

Set Up an Aquarium

IT CAN BE AS LITTLE AS A TINY BOWL with some colored rocks and one little Beta fish, or something more extravagant with several varieties of tropical fish. Watching fish do their thing is another hobby that has been proven to reduce blood pressure and relieve stress.

No wonder then that I've noticed fish tanks filled with beautiful, mesmerizing fish in dentist waiting rooms, hospitals and hospices. Many corporate offices install fish tanks in their lobbies as well.

Keeping fish requires regular, but not really very time-consuming, care. And, another part of the fun of this hobby is learning about the fish you're keeping. Check out on-line resources and books at pet stores to find out more about the fascinating undersea world.

Take Care Tip #90

Beading

WHETHER THEY'RE SPARKLY AND SHINY, or rough and earthy, beads are fun and relaxing to work with. Planning, placing and creating your bead project calls upon motor, visual and cognitive skills. If you're new to the art of beadwork, a very simple project is a wine charm – a clever way to allow your guests to keep track of their water or wine glasses. They just clip right around the stem of the glass and rest at the base.

I'm suggesting this project because you don't have to buy any of the special jewelry-making tools or a ton of different beads. It's a nice, inexpensive way to try it out before you commit to this hobby. Then, if you like it, go crazy at the bead store and try more projects.

What You'll Need To Make Six Wine Charms

- Hoop Earrings: You can get these at any craft store in the bead area. They usually come in packs of six. Choose a thin hoop in gold or silver that has the kind of closure that just hooks together (not the kind with a post, as you need the complete circle).
- Beads: You can buy a package of multi-colored, multi-sized beads for a dollar or two, and you will still have a lot left over after this project.
- Charms: Buy a package of charms that contains at least six different ones, so your guests will be able to tell their glasses apart. (Many are sold in themes for holidays: flowers, leaves, etc.)

How You Do It

Simply open one hoop earring, and thread the beads in the following order: one small bead, one large bead, charm, one large bead, one small bead. Close the earring back up and repeat with the other earrings, beads and charms. Voilà!

Take Care Tip #91

GENEALOGY

WE'RE SO WRAPPED UP in our families anyway, why not spend some time really getting to know our family history? Maybe you're related to a founding father, or royalty. Maybe your family suffered through poverty or slavery. Maybe you are related to an infamous criminal!

Genealogy involves searching for and then using a variety of archived records to trace your family connections. New technology has made it easier than ever to find old birth and death certificates, marriage licenses and property titles that can provide interesting clues to where you came from.

There are plenty of expensive family tree services out there ready to help you, but you don't need to get pulled into any of that. Chances are good you'll be able to get things rolling for free with a call to your city library. Many have people there who are able to help you find family records. You can gather up any names, dates, and family paperwork that you might already have to help with the process, and take them with you. But, really, with just your name, birth date, and the place you were born, the person at the library will be able to help you to find out quite a bit about your relatives. Also, websites like *www.EllisIsland.org* and *www.FamilySearch.org* offer access to their archives for free.

Deciding to pursue genealogy makes you a family detective. You will be able to spend as little as a few minutes, or much longer, reviewing the information you gather. With each discovery, you'll get more information that will help your next search. You can keep chipping away with your own Internet searches. This is another one of those hobbies you can share: think about interviewing older family members to help fill in some of the blanks.

Tracing your family heritage will be fun and exciting, and may even provide a sense of comfort and security as you connect to your own remarkable and deep roots.

nine

Let Me See a Smile

❦

I'VE CARED FOR SOMEONE I LOVED (still love) who was dying. I fully understand that putting on a happy face is not only difficult while you're in a situation like that, it actually seems crazy to even think about.

As I write this book, I'm constantly thinking about all of the different kinds of caregivers who might be reading it. Maybe you're caring for a critically ill child. Maybe your caregiving has been going on for years. Maybe you're caring for someone who is near death. All of those scenarios are horrible. They really are.

It's NORMAL to feel bad about those kinds of things. And it's WRONG to think you must tamp down your feelings and put on a strong face for others. There's another way, a healthier way.

Be honest with yourself

I want to tell you about creating positive thoughts – which is not the same as "being happy all the time." I don't know if it's possible to be happy all the time. Caring for someone you love brings out a big range of emotions.

Let me introduce Anthony Rapp. He's the Broadway star who originated the role of Mark Cohen in *Rent*. He's also a *New York Times* best-selling author of his book, *Without You: A Memoir of Love, Loss, and the Musical Rent*. It includes stories about his days in *Rent*, but also about his mother's long struggle with cancer.

Rapp recently launched a stage version of *Without You* at the City Theatre here in Pittsburgh. I was in the audience and was moved to tears by the heart-felt way he spoke and sang about his mother, and his relationship with her. After the show, I sought him out for an interview for this book, which he graciously agreed to.

Rapp is quick to point out that he was not the day-to-day caregiver for his mother. He was living and working in New York City (exactly where his mother told him she wanted him to be) during much of her illness, but he visited her, spent time with her, and was there to see some of her good days and some of the not-so-good ones.

"There were moments when I felt I lost my mind," Rapp explains. "My nerve endings seemed so exposed, so raw. But I learned something that I want to get across to others through my show: Be honest with yourself, with the anger or whatever you are feeling. That's part of taking care of you. Feeling the anger, the depression, the fear, the resistance – it's all part of it. Any feelings you resist, or deny, or ignore will come back to bite you. What you resist persists."

Through his experience with *Rent*, Rapp was introduced to Friends in Deed, a caregiver support group based in New York *(www.FriendsInDeed.org)*. He now is on the board of directors. Their mission is to help people, and their message is simple: we're all in the same boat. "At Friends," he says, "a person who just lost someone to AIDS could be sitting next to someone caring for someone with cancer. The people who need support are not broken up into categories, and it's set up that way on purpose, so that everyone understands that no one is alone. They may have different specifics involved with their situations, but they are all feeling the same range of emotions."

Thank you, Anthony Rapp.

In this chapter you will see that you can be sad. You can be scared. You can be mad. AND, you can remain positive through it all. You have the power to retrain your brain and turn negative thinking into positive living. Sound impossible? Read on...

But there's so *much* to feel negative about

Sure, there are plenty of days when it seems like it's easier to see the negative side of daily life. With health problems, big bills, too many things and not enough time swirling around you, it can be tough to find some good in all of it ... something to smile about.

The search for something good can feel like a lot of work. One more thing to add to your already overwhelming list. So, you cave. You stop even *trying* to be positive. You let one little bad thing grow bigger and spoil your whole day. Soon, you find yourself grumbling your way from one day to the next – maybe dredging up a "good face" for others, maybe not.

The wildly popular book, *The Secret*, put a spotlight on centuries-old concepts regarding the power of positive thinking. Very simply, it revolves around the idea that thoughts are magnets. So, one negative thought attracts more negative thoughts. Positive thoughts work the same way, but are said to be even stronger. If you ever took a physics class you learned that *like attracts like*. It's the same with our thoughts.

You have the power to decide what magnet you're going to pull out of that brain and use today. Are you fishing for negative thoughts and experiences, or do you want to try to pull in some positive ones? It's all up to you.

Getting your brain to change over to being more positive will take some time. You will probably have moments and days when you slip up. And that's OK as long as you accept that becoming positive is a process, and that it can really work for you. A little bit more every day, and you're there. Before long, thinking about things in a better way will start to just come naturally.

Remember, there are a whole lot of feel-good endorphins in your brain just waiting to be activated!

Where will positive thinking get me?

Believing that you are capable of positive things will help you to achieve positive things. Positive thinking is a great motivator. Negative thoughts hold you back from realizing your full potential. Don't shortchange yourself.

What coach would be worth his salt if he told his team, "Well, the other team looks to be in better condition, and better skilled. They've won more games than we have this season, and I really don't see us being able to beat them. Don't get hurt out there!"

Ha! Can you imagine that happening? No, the coach is in there saying "We have a challenge in front of us today and we are ready for this challenge. We have worked hard for this and now the opportunity is here for us to take it. Let's get out there and do it!"

Those are the kinds of winning attitudes that top business leaders and other successful people speak of. If it works for them, it can work for us. Choosing to have positive attitudes will help you to feel more confident in yourself, and in your abilities to do whatever it is you want to do.

The importance of these kinds of feelings and how to teach yourself to feel them is being studied in a new branch of psychology called *Positive Psychology*. The Positive Psychology Center at University of Pennsylvania was founded by Dr. Martin Seligman, whose research indicates that people have the ability to train themselves to be happier, no matter how they were raised or what is involved in their current life situations.

However, there are doubters out there in the medical community regarding this positive thinking stuff. Can positive thinking directly cause you to be healthier? Some researchers argue that the issue is just too complex to be that cut and dried.

Positive thinking can't hurt you in any way, though. It's not like trying some new experimental pill. So I say, why not try it, and see if you feel the benefits that so many others have.

Getting Started

When we have negative thoughts about something, we react in a negative way. So to get a different response, we need to work on changing the way we're thinking. Over the years, I have interviewed several psychologists regarding positive thinking techniques, and many have suggested that the fastest way to get the brain retraining process started is to replace your negative thoughts with positive ones. Easier said than done, you say? I agree. But the first step in changing something is to recognize that it needs to be changed. So now you're on the first step of the process. You're aware that negative thoughts can get started and you're starting to be alert to them. You're in the game. So here's how it goes:

As soon as you begin to feel a negative thought registering, quickly and actively stop everything and focus on replacing that negative thought with something positive. If you are imagining all of the worst things that could happen, deliberately and consciously tell yourself about all of the best things that will happen. By doing that as quickly as possible, and with consistency, you are helping your brain to adopt that behavior as a habit. Practice that kind of thinking every chance you get, and soon it will start to happen on its own. And your brain will start firing up those delicious-feeling endorphins. What have you got to lose?

What's faith got to do with it? (sometimes a lot!)

I would like to talk about caregiving and spirituality for a moment. At the start of this book I told you that I would freely share my own story with you, in the hope that there might be something you would find helpful in your own life. For me (and I suspect many others), faith and spirituality go hand in hand with positive thinking. And research has shown that people with faith – even it it's simply a belief in a purposeful universe – have an easier time pulling through tough times. Turning to faith in difficult situations has certainly brought me the assurance I needed that "all is well." I speak in this section from my own spiritual point of view, using the words and religious concepts I am most familiar with. Your own frame of reference might be similar to mine or altogether different, but I know that some of these concepts are universal. And so I offer you my thoughts on spirituality and caregiving because maybe they will give you comfort and guidance when things seem bleak

Now, I consider myself a spiritual person, a religious person. I was raised Catholic. Went to a Catholic grade school. Married a Catholic. Our children go to a Catholic grade school. I have always gotten incredible strength from my relationship with God. Most of my caregiving experiences have been rewarding and happy. I truly think of the time with my mother and mother-in-law as an incredible blessing. Plenty of other caregivers feel that way too, I'm sure.

But for others, it's much different. For those with a spiritual bent, sometimes it's hard not to seriously question why God (or the Creator or the Universe) would allow this kind of pain. Are you mad that God would let your loved one suffer? Are you mad at God for putting this burden on you? Are you ashamed that you feel that way? Because maintaining a spiritual connection can offer so much comfort, I think it's important that we talk about that for a little bit – starting with a story of my own.

As I told you earlier, when I got a phone call telling me that my mother had died I instinctively drove to church before I went home to see my family. I didn't set out to make that stop, I was just kind of *drawn* to it. It was weird. I know my first thoughts were of my sisters, and wanting to get to them – to comfort them. But, instead, I remember realizing I was at church without fully knowing how I got there.

Why did that happen? Did the fact that I'm a person who's always been open to seeing and hearing positive signs from God allow me to be pulled exactly where I needed to go? That unplanned visit to church, and the opportunity to hold hands and pray with a nun, gave me the spiritual boost I needed to go home and help my younger sisters and my dad through that time.

When things quieted down a bit after my mom's funeral, I sat at home and prayed. I closed my eyes and told God that I didn't understand why He needed my mother more than I did. I told Him how much I missed her. I needed to know that she was all right, that she would still be able to be with me in some way. I begged for a sign. A movie was on in the room at the time, and just as I glanced up, I saw the image of a white feather floating across the TV screen.

The next morning I woke up still thinking about my mother and my prayer request. When I went out to my car, I noticed something stuck in the driver's door. It was a fluffy white feather.

I have been finding them ever since. Spotting the feathers and picking them up has made me smile, and sometimes cry. They seem to show up in unexpected places just when I am wishing for a hug from my mom. I've told my children a lot about the grandma they never got to meet, and the white feathers; at one time or another each of them has come running to me, smiling and waving a white feather that they discovered!

Scientifically, it has yet to be proven whether prayer has any actual physical bearing on health. Several studies suggest as much, though the methods and findings are still open to debate.

The Rev. Daniel E. Hall, MD, is an Episcopal priest and assistant professor at the University of Pittsburgh. As the first ever Fellow of Religion and Medicine at Duke University, he conducted research on the associations between religion and health. He found that in terms of improved life span, the effect of regular attendance at religious services is about the same as that of regular physical exercise; according to him, both add approximately 3-5 years of life. Dr. Hall explains it this way:

> *The data are still inconclusive, but there is growing evidence to suggest that the religious belief and practice of patients have a concrete, measurable impact on their health and healthcare. Prayer, worship and participation in religious communities not only "improves" health, but it also provides an important way patients weave the experience of illness into their lives in meaningful ways. It is hard to underestimate the power or importance of this in the lives of patients.*
>
> *When my patient asks me "Why did I get colon cancer?" he is not asking for a treatise on the molecular biology of oncogenesis; he is asking an existential question of meaning and value. For many people, the best answer to such questions is expressed in the language of their religious tradition. The best physicians have always understood this, and with great integrity, regardless of their own religious conviction, have offered patients in that existential uncertainty the unique wisdom that they have garnered from caring for others who have wrestled with similar questions.*

This confirms what I've seen in my own life. Can I prove it? No. But I believe my faith has given me special, important tools to make sense of the difficult times. And then there are more of those little "signs." When I've gone out to do my talks on caregiving, it's common for someone in the audience to approach me afterward with a story similar to my white feather story.

Once, a burly, but soft-spoken man shared with me that when he was growing up his father told him that pennies were an angel's way of saying hello. His father suffered an illness and died, and ever since, the man has found shiny pennies in odd, unexpected places, such as the dirty construction sites where he worked. His faith, and those pennies, are what get him through the loss of his dad. Holding onto faith may seem difficult at times, I know. And you may sometimes find yourself in that dark place where nothing gives you solace. In that situation it's easy to feel mad at God. And you know what? My friend Bishop David Zubik says go right ahead. It's OK. It can actually bring you closer to God, and to positive thinking. I discovered why during a recent interview with Bishop Zubik, who leads the Pittsburgh Catholic Diocese.

Along with his many work obligations, Bishop Zubik was a caregiver to his mother for three and a half years as she went through an up-and-down ordeal with cancer. He described that time with his mother as sacred. He shared with me that it made his heart happy to be able to, in some small way, thank his mother for all of the times she comforted him as a child. All the times she quieted his fears.

Bishop Zubik was an only child, and was extremely close to both his parents growing up. He's taking care of his father now. I asked him what he would say to a caregiver who feels a lot of anger towards God. I was surprised at his answer. "Tell Him so," he said, "Yell at Him. Scream that you're mad."

"Seriously?" I asked.

"Yes," the Bishop said. "God can take it."

How beautiful is that? Go ahead and unload. God can take it.

As Catholics, he said, our faith teaches us that God is our Father, so think about parenting situations here on Earth. There are times when your dad's done something to make you mad, sometimes really mad – mad enough to yell horrible things at him. That happens, and he still loves you. And you still love him. It's the same with God. He understands that yelling about a situation is sometimes needed to help to get you through it. So go ahead and yell, but then, as in any relationship you have here, when you're over it and you realize what you've done, you're sorry and you apologize. You might even ask for help. The Bishop guaranteed that God will still love you. And help you.

With that to motivate us, let's get to some easy strategies for positive thinking.

Take Care Tip #92

Put It in Neutral

BEFORE YOU GO WHOLE HOG with changing negative to positive, work on changing negative to neutral. Nurses do this with their patients. They don't hit you with, "How much pain are you feeling?" It's usually more like, "Tell me about your discomfort." The idea behind this is that you shouldn't plant the seed for pain by saying the word "pain."

You can do this as you move through your own day, too. Instead of, "I hate having to wait this long at the doctor's office." Try, "It bothers me to wait so long at the doctor's office." See how that small change takes some of the heat away? See how the first version can make you feel a little more tense about the situation than the second one?

Take Care Tip #93

TO HELP YOURSELF CREATE, accept, and act on positive thoughts, make a promise to yourself that you will try to go to bed and then wake up expecting that only the best will come to you. Believe it with all your heart. It may take a little while to get to that feeling, but be patient. Then, see if you can follow through with little actions, thoughts and language that help to support that belief throughout the day.

Take Care Tip #94

Be Grateful

THERE HAS BEEN MUCH TALK about the benefits of having "an attitude of gratitude." By being thankful for all of the big and little things in your life, you are opening your heart and mind to allow even more good things to come on in.

If you're having a hard time finding something to be thankful for, you can have some fun while getting your brain to respond the way you want it to. Find a part of your body that you're not having any trouble with, and take a few moments to focus on the joy of that. Let yourself get over-the-top, inappropriately happy about it. How's your little finger doing? Is the nail attached? Does it bend where it's supposed to? WOW! You have an awesome little finger! Isn't that great? Nothing wrong there!

As silly as that sounds, psychologists say your brain will pick up on those positive thoughts, and as we've discussed, soon these positive thoughts will come more easily.

Be Proud of Yourself

WHEN YOU'RE NOT FEELING GOOD about yourself, it has a big negative effect on your life as a whole. Having low self-esteem can mean that you miss opportunities because you're afraid to take them. You don't have confidence in your worth, so you don't speak up for yourself, and you don't get what you want.

Start to feel more positive about yourself by accepting compliments – promise yourself that you will simply smile and say thank you the next time someone gives you praise. Recognize your skills and abilities – take stock of them for a few minutes and pat yourself on the back for being you. And avoid all that negative self-talk. Remind yourself that you *deserve happiness and can make positive changes.* Go ahead and stop reading right now and say those words out loud a few times. I'll wait...

You back? Great. Well done. Once you start building good self-esteem, you can watch positive changes unfold.

Love Your Mistakes

THE BIGGEST MISTAKES CAN LEAD to the greatest successes. How does that work? Don't think of a mistake as a failure; think of it as an opportunity to learn.

When you slip up, it's normal to be upset, and maybe a little mad at yourself. Don't stew about it forever though. Think it over, talk about it with friends or family if you want, figure out how you could have avoided the mistake or how you will avoid the mistake in the future, and then let it go. And guess what – the mistake that had you feeling so bad now makes you smarter and stronger. Turn the negative feeling into a positive experience and part of your growth.

Stay on track by knowing that there will be times when you will feel sad or worried. Accept that, and know that it's normal. The key is to make sure you don't ignore those kinds of feelings, or blame yourself for having them as you work through them. The goal is not to be perfect, it's to keep moving forward.

Be Ready

THINK OF POSITIVE THINKING as proactive thinking.

Prepare yourself to react to situations in a positive way by taking some time to look within yourself and figure out your priorities and principles. Ask yourself some questions: What do you believe in? What makes you happy? What are your most enduring values? How would you like the world to see you? What do you absolutely know about yourself (only the positive stuff!)?

By knowing what is at your core, in ten minutes you can create a personal mission statement – just like a business. During the tough times, you'll have your personal mission statement right at hand. It can be your guide, which will make sticking to a positive path even easier.

Positive People Only, Please

I TALKED ABOUT THE IMPORTANCE of seeking out positive people in Chapter 1, and it deserves another mention here. Spending time with, and trying to be like, the most positive people you know is a great way to learn how to be more positive.

Take a few minutes and think about anybody in your family or at work that seems to be really good at keeping it all together. Then, don't be afraid to ask them how they got that way. Are they starting or ending their day with a walk to help relieve stress? Have they made it a point to get to bed a little earlier each night? Chances are good they will be flattered that you noticed their positive ways, and happy to share some tips with you so that you can try them too.

Take Care Tip #99

Positive Protection

USE THE POWER OF POSITIVE VISION to keep your spirits up.

My friend Hannah Keeley, mom of seven (!), TV (and real life) personality, and author of *Total Mom Makeover*, shared this tip with me. She says, "When you get dressed in the morning, imagine that you are clothing yourself in a shield of joy. Things won't always go as you want them to during the day. Frustrating events and irritating people can try to make you upset, but imagine all of that negative energy rolling off your shield. Don't give anyone or anything the power to rob you of your joy. It's yours to keep."

Take Care Tip #100

STAY CONNECTED

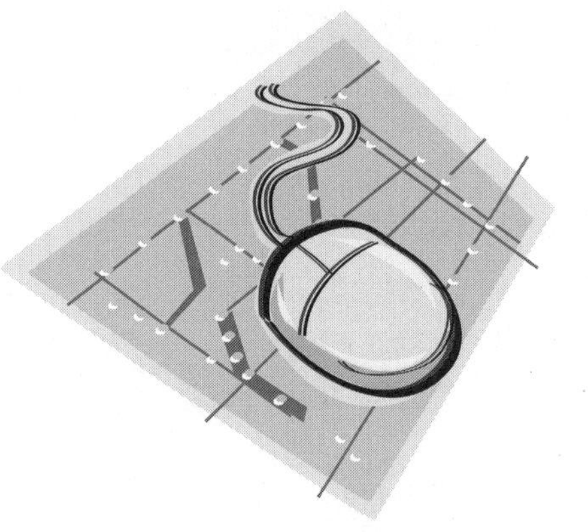

IN CHAPTER 4 I TALKED ABOUT how important reaching out to friends is to alleviate stress.

It's just as vital for staying positive – especially when you feel like you've almost hit bottom. Broadway star Anthony Rapp says that while he was dealing with his mother's cancer, staying connected with friends helped him keep it together. While his mom was sleeping, he would take a few minutes to catch up on his emails or make a quick phone call. Sometimes, he'd talk with friends about how his mother was doing; other times, he'd just listen to things that were going on in his friends' lives.

It's easy to retreat into our own worlds when the going gets tough, but even if we only send a quick note *("Hey – Love ya. It's crazy over here, but let's have coffee soon, 'kay?")*, it's important to keep the friendship channels open. Staying connected helps us keep things in perspective. It reminds us why there's reason for hope.

Take Care Tip #101

SAY A LITTLE PRAYER

BISHOP DAVID ZUBIK TOLD ME that one of the most powerful experiences he had while caring for his sick mother was praying with her every night. We're talking about a Bishop who knows a lot of long, beautifully worded prayers, but he told me he realized that sometimes a lot of words aren't needed.

He and his mother found comfort and strength through the simple prayer, "Jesus, Mary, and Joseph, pray for us." They would repeat that short prayer request several times each night. The Bishop said it helped them both to feel more connected to God, more calm and secure.

You may use these words too if they bring you comfort. Take a moment to think of where you find the most strength in your own faith tradition or belief system. You can easily create your own simple prayer or meditation with whatever words work for you. No need for poetry here – just speak from the heart.

A Prayer for You

No, you don't need a lot of words, or fancy words, to ask for strength and comfort, but sometimes, beautiful words can fill you with hope. Bishop Zubik wrote this Prayer for Caregivers especially for this book. It's his blessing for you:

Dear Father in Heaven,

We ask you to bless the caregivers
who tend to the sick,
the infirm,
the elderly,
and the children,
all those who cannot care for themselves.

We pray that you especially bless
those who are caring for family members.

Help all the caregivers to be strong, patient,
and tender in their ministry.

Lift up their spirits, Lord,
that they may find gladness in their work
and share your joy and peace
with those in their care.

May the healing power of the Holy Spirit
refresh them in mind and body.

Lighten their burdens,
and prepare all of us for that day
when we shall joyfully meet the Great Healer,
your Son, Jesus Christ. AMEN.

Again, no matter what your spiritual beliefs, finding a way to have faith that you are not alone, that a force more powerful than you is able to help you and guide you, can add great positive energy to your life.

A Final Thought from Me to You...

My hope and prayer for you is that you will make the time to nurture the strength you need to make caring for yourself a priority. You are giving so much of yourself, and making lives better as a result. Find the time to reflect on how special that is. Allow yourself to feel pride. Make positive changes to manage the caregiver part of your life, and do everything you can to keep the other important parts of your life alive. Rejoice for the time you have with your loved ones, and for the opportunities you have to be with them to experience life's challenges and blessings.

I hope this isn't goodbye for us. Please keep this book on your shelf and come back to it when you need a little boost in a particular area. Share it with others who become caregivers. I'd love to have you visit me on our web site, too *(www.TakeCareTips.com)*.

Take care!

j.

Resources for Caregivers

FOR MORE TAKE CARE TIPS, information about caregiving and healthy living, and some wonderful products for a happy you, please visit me at *www.TakeCareTips.com.*

There is also a wealth of caregiving information and support on the web. Here are some excellent places to start:

- **The National Family Caregivers Association at *www.NFCACares.org***
- **The National Alliance for Caregiving at *www.Caregiving.org***
- **The National Caregivers Library at *www.CaregiversLibrary.org***
- **Online magazine *Today's Caregiver* at *www.Caregiving.com***
- **American Association of Retired Persons (AARP) at *www.AARP.org/Family/Caregiving***
- **Online caregiving resource site *www.Caring.com***

For mind/body balance and stress-relief information and products, visit Health Psychologist Dr. Nancy Mramor's website at *www.InspiredHealth.info*. Find some of Dr. Mramor's techniques in Take Care Tip # 3 (Better Breathing) and Take Care Tip #11 (Balance Your Brain).

For information on heart health, visit the American Heart Association at *www.AmericanHeart.org*.

For information on walking your way to health, visit fitness expert Leslie Sansone at *www.WalkatHome.com*. Walk at Home is the #1 in-home walking program in the world. Learn about Leslie's ten-minute walking workout in Take Care Tip #22 (Just Walk).

For information on the Food Pyramid and the USDA's Dietary Guidelines, visit *www.MyPyramid.gov*.

For information on sleep and sleep disorders, visit the National Sleep Foundation at *www.SleepFoundation.org*.

To stop junk mail, visit www.OptOutPreScreen.com; to stop those credit card and mortgage offers, visit *www.DMAConsumers.org*. Learn more about these services in Take Care Tip #71 (Get Off the List).

For information on simplifying and managing life, home and work, visit Mary Jo Rulnick, author of The Frantic Woman's Guide to Feeding Family and Friends, at *www.MaryJoRulnick.com*. Find an idea from Mary Jo in Take Care Tip #72 (Clear Your Desk).

For information on organizing and de-cluttering your life, visit organization and motivation expert Meryl Starr at *www.MerylStarr.com*. Find an idea from Meryl in Take Care Tip #75 (Color Coded Closet).

For parenting and healthy living information, visit Hanna Keeley, author of Total Mom Makeover, at *www.TotalMom.com*. Find an idea from Hanna in Take Care Tip #99 (Positive Protection).

If you are living with a life-threatening illness, providing care for someone who is, or if you are grieving the loss of someone in your life, visit Friends in Deed at *www.FriendsIndeed.org*. Learn about Broadway star Anthony Rapp's experience with this wonderful New York-based organization in Chapter 9.

Acknowledgments

THE MESSAGES IN THIS BOOK have been in my head and in my heart for a long time. I am happy for the opportunity to acknowledge and show my gratitude to those who helped these ideas to come out in Take Care Tips:

My mother and mother-in-law, who put me on this path and fuel my passion to help others. I know they are working magic in Heaven to help me. My dad, who encouraged my desire to become an author at age six, and then hand-stitched together my very first book – he has taught me that we each have exactly the amount of strength we need to get through any situation. My grandmothers – for their guidance from Heaven and earth. Becky, Jessica, and Katy – for sending good thoughts to their big sister, and for keeping family a priority. My father-in-law, who brings so much to our lives. My step-daughter, Bethany, for her love and support. My sweet Michael, Alexander, Nicholas, Grace and Joseph – who make me feel like the luckiest Mom in the world everyday; just writing their names makes my heart happy. My husband Joe, who loves and takes care of me – his undying belief in me helps me to believe in myself.

My new St. Lynn's Press family, especially Paul, who cares about his authors as much if not more than he cares about his business. My cross-country Dynamic Duo editing team of Abby and Cathy, who brought incredible wisdom, guidance, humor and warmth to the entire writing process. Holly, for her wonderful work on the text – Jeff, for leading us on a tour of cover designs. And other St. Lynn's authors, for their advice and guidance.

Every person I interviewed for the book, for the gift of their time to talk with me and share information in an effort to help others. My friend, photographer Becky Thurner, who gave her time and talent to capture images to convey the positive feelings and energy we want to send out to caregivers. Bishop David Zubik, and my parish priest, Fr. John Skirtich – for their blessings on this book and our mission to help caregivers. My friend and business mentor Leslie Sansone, for starting me on a walk to a new and exciting journey, and for not ever leaving me alone for too long on this path. My friend Gina and her family, for their gift of love and laughter. My family, friends and neighbors who cheered this project on. My jennifer Productions team, for their constant support.

And God for ... well ... everything.

About the Author and *www.TakeCareTips.com*

❦

JENNIFER ANTKOWIAK spent 17 years as an award-winning TV news anchor and reporter, 14 of which were with the #1-rated news station in Pittsburgh, KDKA-TV (CBS). She currently hosts the popular weekly TV talk show, "jennifer" on Pittsburgh's WTAE (ABC). Jennifer is known not only for her TV work but for her popular multimedia website that offers tips and advice for women *(www.jennifertvshow.com)*. She is the founder of the multimedia company, *jennifer Productions*. In addition to her professional achievements, Jennifer is a wife and mother of five young children and an older step-daughter. She is also a caregiver for her father-in-law, and worked with Hospice to care for her mother-in-law, who recently died of cancer. Jennifer is on a mission to make life easier for women and families.

Her website and blog at *www.TakeCareTips.com* are the online companions to this book.